"'Is the cross, then, an argument?' That pointed question from Nietzsche, with which this work begins, displays an insight into the gospel that its rationalist Christian defenders never attain, as Penner shows with sharp and devastating clarity. Joining his voice to the prophetic words of Kierkegaard, Penner calls us to the *logos* of the cross, to that form of reason whose beginning is crucifixion and whose end is the humble service of the neighbor. This book makes a crucial intervention: for those who have knelt too long before the idol of apologetics or been wounded by it, their healing can begin here."

—**Douglas Harink**, The King's University College, Edmonton

"What is the 'end' of apologetics—defeat or conversion? Myron B. Penner's provocative critique of the 'rhetorical violence' of the 'apologetics industry' needs to be heard especially by apologists, as does his radically alternative model of 'edifying prophetic witness'—a witness that calls for conversation rather than debate and for Christians to embody the truth they profess in their lives rather than merely prove propositions through their arguments."

—**Robert MacSwain**, Sewanee: The University of the South

"Myron Bradley Penner has written that rarest of books: the book that needs to be written. He exposes the fatal flaws of modern Christian apologetics, putting words to the unease many Christian theologians and philosophers have long felt about the apologetic enterprise. But the importance of Penner's book is not merely in its critique of apologetics; even better, it lights a way forward for authentic Christian witness in a postmodern age."

—**Michael W. Pahl**, author of *The Beginning and the End* and *From Resurrection to New Creation*

The End
of Apologetics

Christian Witness in a Postmodern Context

Myron Bradley Penner

Baker Academic
a division of Baker Publishing Group
Grand Rapids, Michigan

© 2013 by Myron Bradley Penner

Published by Baker Academic
a division of Baker Publishing Group
P.O. Box 6287, Grand Rapids, MI 49516-6287
www.bakeracademic.com

Printed in the United States of America

Library of Congress Cataloging-in-Publication Data
Penner, Myron B., 1968–
    The end of Apologetics : Christian witness in a postmodern context / Myron
Bradley Penner.
        pages cm
    Includes bibliographical references and index.
    ISBN 978-0-8010-3598-2 (pbk.)
    1. Apologetics. 2. Witness bearing (Christianity). 3. Postmodernism—Religious
aspects—Christianity. I. Title.
    BT1103.P46 2013
    239—dc23   2013004634

13   14   15   16   17   18   19   7   6   5   4   3   2   1

In memoriam
The Reverend Joseph Walker

Requiem aeternam dona ei, Domine, et lux perpetua luceat ei

Contents

Acknowledgments

For a variety of reasons, this book took an extraordinarily long time to write. Along the way there were many people who edified, encouraged, supported, and continued to believe in it. Without them I would not have finished, and I owe them each a debt of thanks. At the very top of that list of benefactors are my wife, Jodi Penner, and each of our three daughters—Abigail, Sophia, and Isabella. There can be no end of telling of the ways I am blessed by each of them. Their love is the most tangible expression of God's grace I can imagine in this world. My father, Kenneth Penner, also possesses the knack for dropping an encouraging word or timely piece of advice, and his love, along with my mother's (Myrna Penner), is a sustaining force in my life. Next in line for beatification should be Bob Hosack at Baker Academic, who has been long-suffering and faithful to me throughout the process of bringing this manuscript to press, in addition to lending his judiciousness and insight to the project. I am grateful to you, Bob.

Many other individuals and institutions have conspired to support me in a myriad of ways too many to count, and I owe them all my thanks and appreciation, trusting they may be absolved of any responsibility for the shortcomings of this book. Of these, I must express my deep gratitude to The Right Reverend Jane Alexander, Bishop of the Anglican Diocese of Edmonton, my pastor, but also my friend, for her grace and care. Gordon Marion, Cynthia Lund, and the entire staff at the Hong Kierkegaard Library, St. Olaf College, hosted me and provided me with access to their collections, but also welcomed our family into their community and made it possible for me to draft the outline and proposal for the book. I continue to value and count on their friendship. Wayne and Linda Williams (Uncle Wayne and Aunt Linda) allowed me to camp out in their basement and gave me the space and time to draft the bulk of the manuscript. "Thank you" seems an inadequate response to their love and support. I must also thank Archdeacon Michael Rolph and all the parishioners at The Anglican Parish of Christ Church, Edmonton—especially the wardens Lynda Phillips, Martha Watson, Rick Theroux, and Keith Spencer. It has been a joy and privilege to share in the ministry of the gospel with all of you, and to learn further what it means to be a witness to Jesus Christ.

Several of my colleagues in the Diocese of Edmonton also supported me in this endeavor, particularly The Reverends Joseph Walker, Stephen London, and Thomas Brauer. I am also grateful to Mabiala Kenzo for his generosity and support. Many other individuals also talked through or read part or all of the manuscript, offering their advice and insight. Try as they might, they could not correct all its flaws, and they should not be held responsible for any that remain. These include Merold Westphal, Kevin Vanhoozer, Jonathan R. Wilson, John Franke, C. Scott Baker, Douglas Harink and his theology reading group (particularly David Eagle and Jonathan Coutts), Bruce Ellis Benson, Stephen Martin, David Williams, Paul Joosse, Robert Brink, Miles Dyck, Michael Buttrey, Steven D. Martz, and an anonymous reviewer. Finally, I am grateful to Dan Poxon, who listened to my ravings and, in addition to giving me friendship, provided insight and a modicum of sanity to my argument.

Introduction

Against Apologetics

Is the cross, then, an argument?

Nietzsche

Alasdair MacIntyre begins his provocative book *After Virtue* with a "disquieting suggestion." He asks us to imagine that a series of environmental disasters occur around the world and the general public places the blame for them squarely on scientists. Subsequently, natural science itself suffers the effects of this catastrophe. Riots break out across the globe, institutions of scientific research and teaching are destroyed, scientists are lynched and their books, equipment, and instruments destroyed, and all records of their existence expunged.[1] Eventually this reaction matures into a political movement that successfully abolishes the teaching of science from schools and universities. The remaining scientists are locked away so their views cannot infect society.

---

1. As Michael Buttrey pointed out to me, MacIntyre's scenario bears an uncanny similarity to the basic plot of Walter Miller's *A Canticle for Leibowitz*, first published in 1960. See Walter M. Miller Jr., *A Canticle for Leibowitz* (London: Harper Voyager, 2006).

1

Over time, however, a handful of "enlightened" people, who recall the marvels of science, react to this destructive movement. They seek to restore science to its former place, only they possess but a fragmentary knowledge of what it once was: bits and pieces of theories, chapters in books, partial articles, miscellaneous scientific instruments and equipment—all dissociated from the wider practices and theoretical underpinnings from which they arose and in which they originally made sense. Nonetheless, these fragments of science are redeployed within a new set of practices labeled according to the traditional branches of science: biology, chemistry, and physics. People continue to use scientific expressions—such as mass, neutrino, deoxyribonucleic acid, and stoichiometry—systematically and in interrelated ways, yet largely without relation to the manner in which those expressions were used in former times prior to the loss of scientific knowledge.

Accordingly, MacIntyre tells us, "Adults argue with each other about the respective merits of relativity, evolutionary theory, and phlogiston theory, although they possess only a very partial knowledge of each." The children also are taught to engage in these of practices and "learn by heart the surviving portions of the periodic table and recite as incantations some of the theorems of Euclid."[2] The problem is that no one, or almost no one, realizes that they are not practicing natural science properly at all. For, as MacIntyre notes, "everything they do and say conforms to certain canons of consistency and coherence and those contexts which would be needed to make sense of what they are doing have been lost, perhaps irretrievably."[3]

MacIntyre presents this thought experiment in order to introduce his answer to the question of why contemporary discussions of morality are characterized by a fundamental and interminable lack of consensus. There seems to be no way of securing rational agreement regarding moral issues in Western culture.[4] So MacIntyre's controversial thesis is that the moral language of our actual world is in the same state of disorder and chaos that exists in regard to natural

2. Alasdair MacIntyre, *After Virtue: A Study in Moral Theory*, 2nd ed. (Notre Dame, IN: University of Notre Dame Press, 1984), 1.

3. Ibid.

4. Ibid., 6.

science in his imaginary world. What we possess, he believes, are only the *parts* and *pieces* of a coherent worldview and set of practices and *not* anything like a rational community with shared conceptual schemes, concepts, language, and practices that make sense of our perspectives and claims.[5]

According to MacIntyre, the great disaster that erased our knowledge of past moral discourse and put us in this state of grave disorder may be described more or less as the Enlightenment—or perhaps we could say the modern emphasis on universal, neutral (impersonal, ahistorical), and autonomous reason—which cuts off the modern self and its rational grounds for belief from a dependence on tradition or any other source outside the self.[6] There is an immense burden on modern thinkers to vindicate the old rules and practices of morality according to the rationality of free, autonomous, and sovereign moral agents—or else chalk them up to mere individual preference. This burden to justify moral rules in terms of the newly conceived Enlightenment rationality has almost completely failed, MacIntyre believes, and it was always doomed to fail because people no longer share a common understanding of the world or the self.

And it is precisely this feature of the calamity—its fundamental tie to the Enlightenment picture of the world—that renders it invisible to us today. We have no historical record or memory of this intellectual disaster because history to us means *academic* history, with its value-neutral standpoint, which is itself a product of the modern Enlightenment.[7] Once the assumptions of the Enlightenment are accepted, MacIntyre's disaster is rendered virtually invisible, as the results of the Enlightenment cannot be but perceived as good and, even more, as inevitable and "natural."[8] So the degree to which we

---

5. Ibid., 2.
6. To oversimplify, in MacIntyre's assessment, the Enlightenment project conceives of the moral agent as an utterly free self-governing being, sovereign in its moral authority, and yet continues to use the inherited language, rules, concepts, and discourse of morality that found their home in a fundamentally different picture of the self and the world—a world that was designed by God and governed through absolutely binding moral laws. Cf. MacIntyre, *After Virtue*, 63.
7. Ibid., 4.
8. Cf. Charles Taylor: "Once we are well installed in the modern social imaginary, it seems the only possible one, the only one that makes sense. . . . Our embedding

accept the Enlightenment picture of the world and assume its values
is also the degree to which we will be oblivious to the changes our
culture has undergone in the Enlightenment.

Another Disquieting Suggestion

This is a book about apologetics. Or, more precisely, it is a book *against*
apologetics, for what I wish to propose is that what MacIntyre describes
in *After Virtue* regarding moral inquiry is true also of Christian theology
in general, and specifically Christian apologetics.[9] As MacIntyre tells
the story, moral judgments undergo an (almost) imperceptible—but
immensely significant—transformation in modernity. The ancient and
medieval—that is, premodern—habit of making moral judgments as
true or false persists in modernity, but their import and meaning are
completely changed.[10] The result is that moral debates are deadlocked
and interminable, and there seems to be no rational hope of resolving
them in a single point of view. This subtle evolution in moral discourse
occurs in modernity—or so MacIntyre contends—because, on the one
hand, the traditional *language* of moral concepts (such as the normative use of the term "good") and arguments carries on, while, on the
other hand, the traditional conceptual structures and social practices
that gave this language its meaning and sense have been lost.

in modern categories makes it very easy for us to entertain a quite distorted view of
the process [by which we became embedded in those modern categories]." *Modern
Social Imaginaries* (Durham, NC: Duke University Press, 2004), 17.

9. I am not the first to make this suggestion, of course, and other theologians,
such as Stanley Hauerwas at Duke University, have applied MacIntyre's thought to
theology. For a recent and effectual example, see Jonathan R. Wilson, *Living Faithfully in a Fragmented World: From* After Virtue *to a New Monasticism* (Eugene, OR:
Cascade Books, 2010). I should also point out that whether MacIntyre is finally right
or wrong in all the details of his account of our contemporary situation and how we
got here—and even more in the specific prescriptions he offers to our situation—is
beside my point. What I assume is that MacIntyre is fundamentally right about the
dramatic shift to modernity from what preceded it, and that he is essentially correct
in his assertion that this shift hinges on a new conception of human being and the
nature and role of reason. MacIntyre's story is not at all unique to him, and there
is a strong contingent of scholars who agree in the basic movements he traces. For
example, see Charles Taylor's body of work, but especially Charles Taylor, *A Secular
Age* (Cambridge, MA: Belknap, 2007).

10. MacIntyre, *After Virtue*, 58–59.

This means our present situation is far more like that of Alice in *Alice in Wonderland* than it is like that of the crew of the starship Enterprise NCC-1701-D in the television show *Star Trek: The Next Generation*. Unlike Alice, the crew of the Enterprise find themselves in a pluralistic world that is fairly well-defined by a "United Federation of Planets" that, despite differences, is banded together under a common constitution. Their world is also made relatively unambiguous by clear-cut boundaries between discrete species and races within the Federation itself, and by a clear mission[11] and a "Prime Directive"[12] that provide a rubric to make sense of their engagements with races and species outside the Federation. Alice, however, finds herself down the Rabbit Hole, alone in an underground world that in many respects resembles her life top-side, yet in a jumbled and chaotic way that is hard to anticipate. The different beings she encounters underground *appear* in some ways like those above ground and often *sound* the same, as they use the same vocabulary and engage in similar practices (e.g., Alice's "trial" in the court of the Queen of Hearts). The differences are just enough, however, to make everything so confused and muddled that the world inside the Rabbit Hole is barely intelligible to Alice. And the same holds, by MacIntyre's account, for our attempts to make moral sense of ourselves and our world as we seek to ground these in an independent rational framework.

The important point is MacIntyre's insistence that the problem for Western modernity is not pluralism per se, but *fragmentation*.[13] By "pluralism" I mean the coexistence of various rival communities and traditions that are relatively intact and embody (to some extent) self-contained and coherent perspectives that can be distinguished from each other.[14] We assume, when we define our culture as pluralistic, that there exists an underlying and independent rational framework that grounds the contrasting mosaic of the discrete

11. According to Captain Jean-Luc Picard's voice-over in the introduction to each episode, the Enterprise's ongoing mission is "to explore strange new worlds, to seek out new life and new civilizations, to boldly go where no one has gone before."
12. The "Prime Directive" is a mandate not to interfere with the internal development of any civilization.
13. MacIntyre, *After Virtue*, 2. Jonathan Wilson also emphasizes this in Wilson, *Living Faithfully*, 13–18.
14. Wilson, *Living Faithfully*, 16.

perspectives and positions around us. We then proceed to make sense
of who we are, where we are, and how we are to act on that basis.
The trouble is, in our current situation we possess only simulacra of
coherent, rival traditions; the language(s) we use and the practices
in which we engage are all jumbled together and missing important pieces—much like the inchoate discourses Alice encounters
in her underground world. The various conceptual schemes that
are available to us, and which we regularly employ, are fragmented
to the degree that they lack precisely those contexts and practices
that gave them their significance and meaning. Yet we continue, as
Jonathan Wilson notes, to speak, act, and believe *as if* we live in a
pluralistic culture made up of competing outlooks, communities, or
positions that can be reasonably differentiated from each other.[15] We
think we are on the starship Enterprise, but in reality we are down
the Rabbit Hole with Alice. Thus, there is a critical blindness that
accompanies our forgetfulness.

So too, I contend, for apologetics. By and large, apologetic arguments and natural theology are linguistic survivals from the practices
of classical Christianity that have lost the context that made them
meaningful and relevant. Subsequently, as with moral discourse,
modern arguments around the existence of God, God's goodness,
etc., are subject to interminable disagreement and a deep confusion
that stem from their dislocation from a premodern worldview. The
church has carried on its own version of the Enlightenment project
in relation to its foundational discourse and has sought the same
independent, rational justification for the gospel.[16] In the Enlightenment, the modern church inherits a vocabulary about God, the
world, and the self from premodern Christianity in the same way
modern Western culture inherited its moral language—and it faces
the same pressures to justify its beliefs and practices using reasons
that appeal to free, autonomous, and sovereign rational agents. This
Christian apologetic version of the Enlightenment project suffers from
the same substantial problems as does the wider Western cultural
Enlightenment project.

15. Ibid., 16.
16. Cf. ibid., 29.

I should clarify that by "apologetics" I mean roughly the Enlightenment project of attempting to establish rational foundations for Christian belief.[17] I use this loose definition to cover a wide range of apologetic discourses that include both the project of defending the reasonableness of Christian orthodoxy and the broader theological project of articulating a rationally intelligible theology in "objective" and "neutral" terms that those outside the Christian community can accept. In short, I am referring to apologetic theology in both of its modern forms—conservative and liberal.

The hypothesis I wish to put forward is that the current apologetic debates—over the "rational foundations" of Christian theism or faith, reasons or evidences for faith in general, the sensational debates over "the New Atheism," or evolution vs. creation—all share a similar fragmentary nature that produces the same interminable lack of consensus in moral discourse. They are also subject to a similar misfortune with respect to what we might call their conceptual grammar—that is, the language and ideas they employ.[18] When we use the language and arguments of ancient and medieval Christianity today, not only are the issues under contention significantly different, but the language and arguments themselves have actually been transformed from their original discourse. So it is that many attempts to articulate the reasonableness of Christian faith in our context paradoxically end up doing something different than defending genuine Christianity.

17. This way of defining apologetics will be important for what follows, as it does not refer to apologetics *simpliciter*, whose minimal concern is to defend Christian faith from specific charges of "falsehood, inconsistency, or credulity." Steven B. Cowan, introduction to *Five Views on Apologetics*, ed. Steven B. Cowan (Grand Rapids: Zondervan, 2000), 8. I am not, in other words, against pointing out where a given challenge to Christian belief is flawed or highlighting how it is that Christianity makes good sense of the world. However, as should be clear in what follows, the discourse of modern apologetics inevitably engages in apologetics in the sense I reject, even (or especially) when it claims to be doing apologetics *simpliciter*.

18. Unlike MacIntyre, however, whose project is to make the reasons for the demise of moral discourse universally intelligible—"to radicals, liberals and conservatives alike" (MacIntyre, *After Virtue*, 4)—by way of a thoroughly historicist recounting of our cultural situation, my project assumes all this as a working hypothesis and aims at redescription on this basis. That is to say, I am not going to perform a historicist re-working of the rise of modern apologetics in MacIntyre's style. He wants to *argue* for his view of the world; I want to give a different account of it.

Despite its usefulness, I do not wish to overplay the analogy between MacIntyre's metaphor and the situation facing apologetics.[19] The chief feature I mean to highlight is that *speaking and thinking about God in our modern culture is fundamentally different from doing so prior to the Enlightenment*. And what is more, the modern Enlightenment worldview, while perhaps not quite arbitrary, is nevertheless just *one way* of seeing the world—including its views of reason, knowledge, and truth—and not the preordained result of inevitable progress or the unimpeachable acme of human achievement. Unless this point is explicitly acknowledged—if we *forget* this—we have a corresponding blind spot in our perspective that can have devastating results. We will have a theology (and Christian witness) fraught with deep conceptual confusions that fails, to that degree, to make Christian practices intelligible—or be *truly* Christian.

Undoubtedly, many of my readers believe apologetic discourse to be the very heart of Christian thought and the means by which Christianity is demonstrably true, intellectually satisfying, and worthy of belief, or has anything relevant to say to us today at all. What could be more obvious—to Christians, at least—than the value of apologetics? Is not defending Christian belief whenever it is challenged, refuting all contrary viewpoints, and establishing its rational foundations a crucial part of Christian witness and in fact a Christian duty? And, we might add, why should one not profit from this by generating an entire industry around this effort, commodifying it so that this "Good News" can reach as many people as possible?

John Stackhouse issues a timely admonition in his helpful book *Humble Apologetics*. Acknowledging Christians often lack a desirable humility regarding their convictions and realizing they are frequently prone to overestimate the rational warrant for their beliefs, Stackhouse warns that apologetics can be both blessing and curse.[20]

19. My approach in this book is fundamentally different than MacIntyre's attempt to recover what is procedurally a premodern form of rationality (cut off from its ontological and metaphysical moorings in a premodern cosmology) that is able in principle to be the final (albeit contingent) arbiter of belief. Instead, I wish to position human reason in a more explicitly after-modern way that lacks the exalted status MacIntyre gives his tradition-based concept of reason.

20. John G. Stackhouse Jr., *Humble Apologetics: Defending the Faith Today* (Oxford: Oxford University Press, 2002), xi.

Defending Christian belief is not an unqualified good; it may actually be counterproductive to faith. There are times and ways in which a given "defense" of the faith does more harm than good to the cause of Christ. Stackhouse certainly points us in the right direction, but my unsettling proposition above forces us to radicalize his conclusion: not only *can* apologetics curse; it actually *is* a curse. Here I take my cue from Søren Kierkegaard, the nineteenth-century Danish philosopher and theologian, who stipulates that the one who came up with the idea of defending Christianity in modernity is a second Judas who *betrays* the Christ under the guise of a friendly kiss; only, he adds, the apologist's treachery (unlike Judas's) is "the treason of stupidity."[21] Kierkegaard's[22] claim about modern apologists makes sense, I believe, if we understand him to be proposing in apologetics something like the scenario MacIntyre describes regarding the contemporary language of morals and morality. According to Kierkegaard, contemporary apologists use Christian vocabulary in a confused and contradictory manner. They use language that performs the opposite of its intended function, and therefore actually betray Christianity rather than defend it.[23] When we place this critique of apologetics alongside MacIntyre's

21. Søren Kierkegaard, *Sickness Unto Death*, ed. and trans. Howard V. Hong and Edna H. Hong (Princeton: Princeton University Press, 1980), 87. To be fair to Kierkegaard, and more accurate, I should acknowledge Kierkegaard's pseudonym "Anti-Climacus" as the one who makes the above assertion, rather than Kierkegaard himself. For a variety of reasons, Kierkegaard uses pseudonyms to write several books and requests that we do them—and him—the honor of citing the pseudonyms, rather than Kierkegaard himself, whenever they are quoted. It is true, however, that Kierkegaard makes almost exactly the same claims about apologetics in the writings he signed, including his personal journals and papers. It is also important to note—for reasons that should become apparent in chap. 2—that the text quoted earlier actually says that the first one to come up with the idea of defending Christianity *in Christendom* is a "Judas No. 2."
22. As I just noted, it is Anti-Climacus who is the "author" of the text in question. However, from now on I will use "Kierkegaard" as shorthand for the authors of all and any of the ideas contained in the texts published by "Søren Kierkegaard," whether pseudonymous or not. This is done only for sake of clarity and convenience and not to ignore the significance of Kierkegaard's pseudonymity or the challenges it poses for interpreting his texts.
23. Unlike Peter Rollins, whose position I often find opaque, I am not thinking here of betrayal as a virtue. See Peter Rollins, *The Fidelity of Betrayal: Towards a Church Beyond Belief* (Brewster, MA: Paraclete Press, 2008).

thought experiment, it appears that something catastrophic occurred in the Enlightenment continues to affect not only our current beliefs, practices, and language concerning morals, but also our current beliefs, practices, and language concerning Christianity. Something else happens when we place Kierkegaard's thought alongside MacIntyre's. We are given a new way of moving forward from modernity. In light of the failure of the modern project, MacIntyre's analysis brings us to a juncture where we are forced to *either* follow Nietzsche's nihilism, which embraces the failure of the Enlightenment project while retaining its fundamental shift away from premodern views of self, the world, and reason, *or* follow Aristotle's tradition-centered form of practical reason that is rooted in the narrative of a community and embodied in identifiable virtues and practices. I see Kierkegaard as offering us a middle way of sorts. He accepts something like a Nietzschean critique of modernity, yet he does so in terms of the Christian categories of revelation, incarnation, sin, conversion, repentance, faith, hope, and love.[24] The values of tradition, community, and so on remain open to modernity, but they are relative to God's revelation to us in Jesus Christ.

I have no doubt some might be tempted to dismiss my thesis out of hand simply because of my Kiergaardian starting point. Kierkegaard's rejection of apologetics is not new news, after all. It is somewhat of a standard requirement in introductory apologetics courses to be able to fashion a response to Kierkegaard's alleged *fideism*—a view that sees faith and reason as fundamentally opposed to each other, and in matters of faith rejects reason altogether in a so-called leap of faith to embrace the absurd.[25] This is in fact MacIntyre's assessment of Kierkegaard as well, and it leads him to believe Kierkegaard has nothing substantial to offer us beyond yet another version

24. I develop this reading of Kierkegaard more in Myron B. Penner, "Kierkegaard's Critique of Secular Reason," in *The Persistence of the Sacred in Modern Thought*, ed. Chris L. Firestone and Nathan A. Jacobs (Notre Dame, IN: University of Notre Dame Press, 2012), especially 379–86.

25. For an extremely influential rendering of this view of Kierkegaard, see Francis A. Schaeffer, *Escape from Reason* (London: Inter-Varsity Fellowship, 1968), 46, 51.

of Nietzsche's nihilism.[26] However, my thought-experiment is built on the premise that Kierkegaard's point will be incomprehensible from the standpoint of modernity. This means the typical treatment of Kierkegaard as a fideist is not quite accurate—or at least it is not the way I wish to read Kierkegaard. The trouble I have with the fideist reading of Kierkegaard—in addition to being an inaccurate rendering of what the Kierkegaardian texts actually seem to say—is it continues to treat his thought under the categories of modern philosophy, which he so obviously labored to oppose. Kierkegaard's rejection of apologetics (and its use of reason) is to be seen as part and parcel of his rejection of the *modern* conception of reason—not of reason altogether. This signals a Kierkegaardian way forward that does not entail going back to Aristotle.

It might also seem to some readers that my working hypothesis is wildly fantastic and implausible, if for no other reason than I am claiming only a few Christians are even able to recognize their situation at all.[27] But this is no real objection at all, for, as MacIntyre notes, if our respective hypotheses are true at all, they will certainly appear false initially. That is exactly the situation we propose. So I persist with my suggestion that the language—more to the point, the theoretical presuppositions—we use to defend Christianity is crippled by a debilitating forgetfulness that remains blind to its basic assumptions and is out of line with its own deepest impulses, to the point it cannot speak to our contemporary situation and in the end betrays what it tries to protect.

This places Christian thought and language in a tight spot, though. What is the status of Christian thought if the apologetic foundations of Christian discourse are abandoned? Or, to ask the question differently, what does faithful witness to Jesus Christ look like in a

26. MacIntyre's label for Kierkegaard is "emotivist," as his subject matter is the relation of reason to morality, not to faith. See MacIntyre, *After Virtue*, 39–45. I respond to MacIntyre in Penner, "Kierkegaard's Critique of Secular Reason." I deal with the place of reason in apologetics more in chap. 2.

27. Cf. MacIntyre, *After Virtue*, 4. I am in a better situation in this regard than MacIntyre, who published *After Virtue* in 1981. Since then there have been abundant critiques of modernity and its cognates, and there is a much higher level of recognition of their truth and the corresponding need for humility and charity in Christian belief.

postmodern context? I cannot expect to address these questions exhaustively and in all their complexity. However, I believe Kierkegaard's disavowal of apologetics is particularly relevant to Christians today. I want to explore the possibility Kierkegaard might be right; I want to take seriously his claim that apologetics *itself* might be the single biggest *threat* to genuine Christian faith that we face today. This book, therefore, tries to make sense of the idea that the modern apologetic enterprise so many Christians engage in is a bankrupt venture, a kind of false messiah, and considers what this might mean for Christian witness and discourse.

Changing Paradigms

If my apologetic version of MacIntyre's "disquieting suggestion" is correct, and Kierkegaard is right to describe apologetic efforts as a betrayal of Christianity, Christians will need not merely to have a humbler apologetics, in which they say the same things, make the same arguments with the same basic goals—only in a nicer way. Instead, Christians need *an entirely new way of conceiving the apologetic task.* As I will argue in the next chapter, the only way to describe this is in terms of a major shift in Christian discourse from a modern apologetic paradigm to one that can be characterized as "postmodern." Christian thinkers rarely reflect on the validity of the apologetic enterprise itself, except to argue over aspects of apologetic methodology and postmodernism—*how* we defend Christianity against postmodernity, the status of faith in relation to reason, the role of evidence, and so on. However, the "value-neutral viewpoint"[28] adopted in modernity means my Kierkegaardian perspective on apologetics will remain invisible to it. If we are going to go forward with my hypothesis, then we will have to adopt another, more radical paradigm—one that recognizes and accounts for the blind spots of modernity. What we need, I contend, is a mode or form of discourse about apologetics that is "after modernity," not in the (deeply modern) sense of *overcoming* modernism, or moving *past* it, but one that *copes* with the entrenched problems it produces in both our practical

28. This is MacIntyre's terminology in *After Virtue*, 4.

and theoretical lives. It is in this sense I am advocating a shift to a postmodern paradigm.[29]

I should make a quick comment or two about how I use the term "postmodern." First, I see postmodernity as a kind of self-reflexive condition that emerges as modernity becomes conscious or aware of itself as modernity. The kinds of shifts described by the terms "modern" and "postmodern" are descriptive of material conditions and are directly linked to changes in our social and discursive practices. It makes little sense to think of the postmodern ethos as characterized by a set of theses or adherence to philosophical doctrines and positions. Postmodernity is a *condition*, or a set of attitudes, dispositions, and practices, that is aware of itself as modern and aware that modernity's claims to rational superiority are deeply problematic. So when I refer to Kierkegaard as "postmodern," I mean it in the sense just described. At any rate, I appropriate Kierkegaard here as a Christian thinker who recognizes that modernity posits a new situation for Christian thought (and being) that must be reckoned with on its own terms. And then modernity must be gotten *past*—but not without going *through* it first. Modernity is, for better or worse, our situation, and we may never fully leave it behind us, however much we recognize its inadequacies.[30]

In this book, then, I aim to be Kierkegaard*ian*, even while I do not attempt to write a book on Kierkegaard's views on apologetics per se. Kierkegaard functions as a guiding light, so to speak, who charts the course and provides a good deal of the back story for my approach to apologetics here. You will find Kierkegaard shows up in many important places in the book—not as an authority who settles issues

29. Here it is interesting to note and helpful to reflect on Jean-François Lyotard's comment that postmodernism is "undoubtedly part of the modern," and that "a work can become modern only if it is first postmodern. Postmodernism thus understood," Lyotard continues, "is not modernism at its end but in the nascent state, and this state is constant." *The Postmodern Condition: A Report on Knowledge*, trans. Geoff Bennington and Brian Massumi (Minneapolis: University of Minnesota Press, 1984), 79.

30. I want to avoid the impression that mine is a nostalgic hankering for premodernity, which, as I see it, is problematic as well. The material conditions that gave rise to modernity testify to the inability of premodern views of the world to sustain themselves any longer.

and ends discussions, but more as a sage who offers us wisdom and shapes our deliberations. His awareness of the modern situation and his perceptive diagnosis of the spiritual malaise of modernity make Kierkegaard one of us—our contemporary—and confirm him as a distinctly *post*modern thinker. Kierkegaard lives and writes at the height of the Enlightenment. He is steeped in the cultural and intellectual milieu of his day and finds himself caught up in the modern situation, with its problems and challenges—and he is fully aware of modernity as his general context. What qualifies his critique of apologetics as postmodern is it is part of his critique of modern thought as a whole. As a result, I put Kierkegaard to work to provide me with the basic framework from which I seek to address the issue of apologetics after modernity.

This book, then, is about the status of Christian belief in a postmodern context; it is about the meaning and significance of our Christian talk about God in postmodernity and the conditions in which we believe it and recommend it to others for belief. Rather than *arguing* for the superiority of postmodernism, I assume postmodernism as a starting point and try to make this standpoint intelligible through a technique similar to what Richard Rorty calls *redescription*.[31] Instead of tackling the modern apologetic paradigm head-on and refuting its foundational premises, I want to redescribe the terrain of apologetics so that our blind spots—or at least some of the more glaring ones—are made visible.[32] As Rorty might say, this is an intellectual practice that is necessary when one attempts to radically transform or replace a rigid but widely accepted vocabulary—particularly when one does not want to collapse back into the semantic categories of the contested vocabulary. So, in Rortian (and Kierkegaardian) fashion, my strategy is to try to make the modern apologetic paradigm look bad by using different metaphors than those it employs and, in a sense, by changing the subject in the hope

31. Richard Rorty, *Contingency, Irony, and Solidarity* (Cambridge: Cambridge University Press, 1989), 8–9.
32. Of course, I am keenly aware that every position—mine included—has its blind spots. Blind spots, however, are less of a problem if one's position expressly acknowledges their reality and builds this possibility into its analyses. A major problem with the modern paradigm, as I will explain, is its extreme difficulty in doing just that.

that I might outflank objections by painting a picture that resonates deeply with Christians.[33]

Part of my reason for starting this way is that even if it were possible to *prove* my position (or any other well-developed philosophical paradigm) to all comers (which I am quite sure is *not* possible), I have grave doubts over the value of the exercise. For one, it requires I adopt the language and viewpoint of modernity, which is just the thing I am trying to avoid. My goal is to reorient the discussion of Christian belief and change a well-entrenched vocabulary that simply does not work anymore, whatever its past uses might have been. But my motivation for this project is not (perhaps like Rorty's) merely to change the discussion to keep things "interesting" in a trivial sense. The deepest reason I have for engaging this project is in service of *the truth* and for the sake of the gospel of Jesus Christ. So my incentive comes from a deep conviction that the modern apologetic paradigm does not have the ability to witness *truthfully* to Christ in our postmodern situation. This means I will have much to say about truth later on in this book.

In the next chapter, "Apologetic Amnesia," I attempt to spell out a little more concretely what I mean by "the modern apologetic paradigm" and redescribe it so it stands in stark contrast to the type of postmodern perspective I will propose. The modern apologetic

33. Cf. Rorty, *Contingency, Irony, and Solidarity*, 44. This is also the task John Milbank sets for so-called Radical Orthodoxy in *Theology and Social Theory: Beyond Secular Reason* (Oxford: Blackwell, 1990). Milbank seeks to counter "secular modernity" by putting forward an alternative "*mythos*" or story that is equally unfounded but nevertheless embodies a vision of the world that is attractive (cf. 1, 279). One of the marked differences between Milbank's and my projects is his attempt to articulate a systematic account of a theo-*logos*—a fully developed theological account of human knowledge and secular modernity. Not only am I less ambitious than Milbank, I am also less optimistic regarding the possibility and value of such an account. For a helpful summary of Milbank and radical orthodoxy on this issue, see James K. A. Smith, *Introducing Radical Orthodoxy: Mapping a Post-secular Theology* (Grand Rapids: Baker Academic, 2004), especially 179–82. Smith also reports in *Introducing Radical Orthodoxy*, 180n110, that at a session of the American Academy of Religion in Atlanta, November 2003, Rorty himself asserted the basic similarity between his own redescriptive project and that of Milbank. For an important critical engagement with Milbank (and Radical Orthodoxy) from a Kierkegaardian perspective that is similar to mine, see Justin D. Klassen, *The Paradox of Hope: Theology and the Problem of Nihilism* (Eugene, OR: Cascade Books, 2011).

paradigm, I submit, is embedded in what Charles Taylor calls our modern "condition of secularity." Modern apologetics imagines itself in modern terms to be engaged in an objective, rational discourse outside of political power and other biases, so it may present the untarnished (and objective) truth about things. The goal is fundamentally epistemological—to provide rational warrant (or justification) for the beliefs of believers. The trouble with this is it includes a kind of blindness to the philosophical commitments that shape its perspective.

In chapter 2 ("Apologetics, Suspicion, and Faith") I set out to outline a Kierkegaardian perspective[34] on apologetics—a reading of Kierkegaard's thought that provides us with some resources for apologetic discourse in a postmodern paradigm. I begin by reading Kierkegaard's critique of apologetics through his distinction between a genius and an apostle, and argue that this gives us a perspective from which to establish a Kierkegaardian critique of the modern epistemic paradigm. Several important points come to light in this reading, but one particularly important feature that emerges is its so-called hermeneutics of suspicion, which then becomes the vantage point from which a postmodern critique of apologetics is performed. In other words, Kierkegaard's distinction between a genius and an apostle anticipates Marx's critique of modern reason in terms of ideology; for what happens when the genius is the authority, Kierkegaard observes, is that justification or what counts as "reasonable" in a society is the opinion or perspective of the dominant group, the "established order." This really is a roundabout way of describing what Nietzsche calls *nihilism*, because in this situation God effectively is dead: he can only enter into our rational systems on our terms. When apologetics implicitly functions within the genius model of modernity, it actually becomes another expression of this nihilism. So I suggest what we need is an entirely different model of apologetics than that of the modern epistemological paradigm. We need to shift from an epistemological focus on the rational justification of Christian beliefs to a hermeneutics concerned with explicating and understanding the life of faith.

34. I say "Kierkegaardian" because this perspective is inspired and informed by a close reading of Kierkegaard's texts and not because I claim to present Kierkegaard's personal views.

Chapter 3 ("Irony, Witness, and the Ethics of Belief") links the possibility of a postmodern apologetics to the concept of irony. Rather than framing the issue in terms of an apologetic defense of Christian belief, I prefer to consider a postmodern apologetics in terms of the concept of *witness*—a *prophetic* witness, to be clear—for it orients us to the task differently and generates a completely different set of goals. Here edification—or building up the self—replaces "winning the argument" as the goal of Christian witness (apologetic discourse). This type of postmodern Christian witness is sensitive to the fragility of faith in our secular condition. It is not focused on a defense of the propositional truth of Christian doctrine, but performs an ironic poetics of truth. What we discover is that the shift away from the (modern) epistemology of belief as the paradigm for Christian witness toward a hermeneutics of belief also opens up an *ethics* of belief that, in turn, deepens the critique of modern epistemology. *How* we believe—not just *what* we believe—is important to our belief being justified.

But what of this notion of a "poetics of truth"? What sense can we give that? And how in postmodernity can there be any substantial talk of truth once we have adopted a hermeneutical perspective?

In chapter 4 ("Witness and Truth") I further clarify the approach to truth involved in my Kierkegaardian account of Christian witness and relate it to propositional truth. I begin by noting that the goal of traditional apologetics is to justify the objective truth of the propositions of Christian doctrine. Christianity, the "essentially Christian," is therefore assumed, implicitly or explicitly, to be captured in these propositions. The Christian truths defended by such modern apologetics are taken to be ahistorical, unsituated, abstract, and universal. I then use Kierkegaard's concept of truth as subjectivity to launch a critique on apologetic propositionalism and to provide an alternative way to think about Christian truth. To possess Christian truth is always to *confess* it to be true, to *win* its truth existentially for oneself. This is not a disavowal of the cognitive content of Christian witness; it is a shifting of our perspective about a given truth claim so we think of it in terms of what Paul Ricoeur calls "attestation." As I develop it, this account of truth and truth-telling is *agonistic*—it involves a struggle to stake our truth claims and make them true of us. Christian truth, then, often involves suffering on the part of the witness, and martyrdom—the act of laying down one's life—is the ultimate form of testimony to the truths that edify us.

In chapter 5 ("The Politics of Witness") I connect the ethics of belief (chapter 3) with an ethics of witness, which gives us the resources to attest to Christian truths in a way that is sensitive to a person's particular cultural and social location and does not perpetrate injustice in the name of Christian truth. Here I expose the possibilities of violence in Christian apologetic discourse at both the personal level (when apologetic arguments are used to treat their interlocutors as the "faceless unbeliever") and the social level (when Christian apologetic practice merely reinforces and defends a given set of power relations operative within an unjust social structure). In this latter situation, Christian apologetics ends up reinforcing the dominant ideology in a society and the gospel loses its ability to confront the culture in a prophetic sense. In contrast to this, the postmodern prophetic witness that I advocate is "person-preserving" and involves Gabriel Marcel's concept of sympathy, which propounds a fundamental concern with others as *persons*, not things. This is a noncoercive form of witness that is itself a form of ideology critique, of both the culture within which it is embedded and the Christian subculture out of which it emerges.

This form of witness is *political* in two ways. First, it is political in the deep sense that Christian witness never occurs in a so-called public square free from political power. The prophetic witness understands St. Paul's concept of "the powers" that actively shape and influence us as individuals. The witness, then, brings private commitments into the imagined "public" space and places into question the institutional and political powers that form our identities and relationships. Second, prophetic Christian witness is political in that it requires a church —a community of people who embody the truths professed by Christians through their practices. This is what makes it possible for people to understand and believe the Christian gospel.

The person-preserving aspect of Christian witness comes from its specific form as *agapē*, an aspect of loving one's neighbor. In chapter 5 I introduce the Kierkegaardian notion that the Christian concept of neighbor entails that my neighbor is the one for whom I am infinitely responsible, to whom I have an infinite debt, and whose subjectivity I cannot violently erase. This is an even more radical concept of indebtedness to the other than we have from Emmanuel Levinas and his emphasis on "the face" of the other. In the victory of love, Kierkegaard notes, one is forever fighting on the side of the neighbor against oneself and one's own tendencies to dehumanize and objectify others. This opens up for us an option not considered by Alasdair MacIntyre, who thinks of reason as tradition-based. The temptation for Christians is to think that because there are intelligible reasons for faith within the Christian tradition, this can be a substitute for our reliance on God and our need to hear from him. Instead, I want to say the way reason relates to prophetic witness is *apocalyptic*, in the sense that such a witness emphasizes the dependence of reason on God's action, which disrupts and subverts our attempts to ground it rationally. Prophetic witness, then, always calls its tradition back to its founding event or truth that undoes and reorients everything—including us.

I am writing this book from the vantage point of a member of the Christian community—the church—and I write it for my own edification as well as that of the church catholic. This is therapy as well as theory. I trust it will be obvious that, while I am engaging in a polemic against a certain form of Christian apologetic discourse, my ultimate goal is to open a pathway for faithful witness, not to close down its possibility. As Jacques Derrida noted that his deconstructive project was a labor of love,[35] so too this book is written to build up, not (just) tear down. My hope is the exhortative function of this book will speak also to those who profess no faith—a word of woe to (some of) those within the church, and a word of witness to those outside it.

35. Derrida declares, "I love very much everything that I deconstruct in my own manner; the texts I want to read from a deconstructive point of view are texts that I love." Jacques Derrida, *The Ear of the Other: Otobiography, Transference, Translation*, ed. Christie McDonald, trans. Peggy Kamuf (Lincoln: University of Nebraska Press, 1985), 87.

1

Apologetic Amnesia

> When we suffer from amnesia, every form of serious authority for faith is in question.
>
> Walter Brueggemann

Perhaps the best way to introduce what I mean by the modern apologetic paradigm is to illustrate it with a story. William Lane Craig is one of the more prominent and prolific Christian apologists, and he possesses an impressive array of academic credentials and accomplishments. He is a first-rate analytic philosopher, author, debater, and popular speaker. Craig opens his defense of his "classical" method of apologetics with a personal story of how he came to this methodology for defending the Christian faith—which Craig assumes is the method used by earlier Christian apologists who emphasized "natural theology."[1] In many ways, the story he tells is the same one I want to tell about modern apologetics in general, as his narrative embodies three features of the modern epistemological paradigm of contemporary apologetics I wish to highlight in this

1. William Lane Craig, "Classical Apologetics," in *Five Views on Apologetics*, ed. Steven B. Cowan (Grand Rapids: Zondervan, 2000), 26–28.

chapter: (1) the disembedding of modern individuals from premodern ways of understanding themselves and the world that (2) gives rise to a new view of reason and (3) engenders new, distinctly modern forms of Christianity.

A Tale of Modern Apologetics

Craig's story, as he puts it, hinges on "the age-old issue of the relationship between faith and reason."[2] He confesses that for many years of his Christian life, this issue greatly perplexed him. He came to faith not because of "careful consideration of the evidence" but because of the quality of the lives of a group of Christians who shared the message of their faith with him. But as a teenage convert to Christianity, Craig was eager to share his new faith and immediately began to present arguments for becoming a Christian to his friends and family. He brought this evangelistic enthusiasm with him as he entered a well-known evangelical Christian college, expecting he would learn more arguments to bolster his evangelistic efforts. Instead, this particular college, he tells us, was characterized by a "theological rationalism" that encouraged students "to follow unflinchingly the demands of reason wherever it might lead." To Craig's dismay, the Bible courses he took at this college completely ignored evidences for the historical reliability of the Gospels, and he was taught in theology courses that none of the classical arguments for God's existence were sound.[3]

This did not sit well with Craig, and he even began to question whether he was a true intellectual. He recounts how "frightened and troubled" he was when one of his theology professors remarked that he would renounce Christianity if he could be persuaded of its unreasonableness. This fear led to outright alarm as Craig discovered extremely intelligent students were leaving behind Christian faith in the name of reason. His encounter with Jesus Christ was so genuine

2. See Craig, "Classical Apologetics," 26–27, for this story.
3. This might sound as if Craig is contradicting himself—that his professors are "theological rationalists" but do not ground their beliefs about the Bible and God on reason. What Craig might mean is that the professors at this college were willing to concede that the Bible was historically inaccurate (and therefore not inspired?) and that belief in God was not an article of reason (but of faith?).

and real, and his experience with Jesus had invested his life with such significance, that Craig simply could not throw it all away just because it was deemed irrational. "If my reason turned against Christ," Craig told one professor, "I'd still believe."

And so Craig went through what he describes as "a temporary flirtation with Kierkegaardian fideism." As he understands Kierkegaard to say, Christianity is decidedly anti-intellectual: one is to believe Christianity *because* it is absurd.[4] This is a position, however, Craig could not maintain. He was rescued from Kierkegaard, he tells us, by reading. Two books in particular were important. First, E. J. Carnell's *Introduction to Christian Apologetics* convinced Craig that "reason might be used to show the systematic consistency of Christian faith without thereby becoming the basis of faith." Second, Stuart Hackett's *Resurrection of Theism* stunned him by demonstrating there were, after all, persuasive arguments for God's existence. In addition, Craig notes that popular apologetics books like Josh McDowell's *Evidence That Demands a Verdict* made it obvious to him that "it was possible to present a sound, convincing, and positive case for the truth of Christian theism." So ended his dalliance with the Kierkegaardian notion that faith might be grounded in something other than reason.

However, because of his experience at college with people who lost their faith due to their confidence in reason, Craig still was not able to completely embrace the view that rational arguments and evidence constitute the essential foundation of faith—that is, until he hit upon a new scheme to describe the relationship between faith and reason, "namely, the distinction between *knowing* Christianity to be true and *showing* Christianity to be true." He explains:

> The proper ground of our *knowing* Christianity to be true is the inner work of the Holy Spirit in our individual selves; and in *showing* Christianity to be true, it is his role to open the hearts of unbelievers to assent and respond to *the reasons we present*.[5]

4. Craig, "Classical Apologetics," 27. For more on Craig's reading of Kierkegaard, see William Lane Craig, *Reasonable Faith: Christian Truth and Apologetics*, 3rd ed. (Wheaton: Crossway, 2008), 69–70.

5. Craig, "Classical Apologetics," 28 (my emphasis).

In Craig's view, in order for me actually to *know* something, I must first have a belief about it; then my belief must actually be true; and finally that belief must be justified or warranted for me—so it is rationally appropriate for me to believe it.[6] Because genuine Christian believers have the witness of the Holy Spirit, not only are their beliefs in God true, but they are also always justified or warranted for them—whether or not they have evidence or a good argument to support it. Their belief, therefore, properly counts as knowledge *for them*. But appealing to this epistemic status[7]—or the way in which the belief is properly justified for them—does not make it so *for others* and is not a rational way to persuade others. So, speaking practically, the distinction between knowing Christianity is true and showing it to be true means that rational apologetics is required for the latter, while the former—which depends upon the inner testimony of the Holy Spirit—is the requirement for individuals to have good or proper faith. In other words, Craig believes he has hit upon a way of explaining how Christian faith is rational and genuine knowledge for a person, even when they come to faith through a means other than evidence and arguments—such as his own Christian conversion. By his account, God's action to convince me of the truth of the gospel is *itself* a rational activity—but only for me. Rational argument and evidence will confirm this for me and then demonstrate (or show) the truth of my Christian faith to the unbelieving world.

Craig further explains that the goal of his apologetic effort—and all Christian apologetics—is to end the "epistemic standoff" between the believer and unbeliever by showing Christianity to be true.[8] This

---

6. This is a rough characterization of Craig's account of knowledge, which he gives in *Reasonable Faith*, 41–43. Craig's full account engages the work of Alvin Plantinga and is more philosophically nuanced than my rendering here.

7. "Epistemology" (to which the term "epistemic" is related) is the branch of philosophy that inquires into the nature of knowledge. "Epistemic status," then, refers to the standing that a person's belief has once the standards or norms for knowledge have been applied to it. A positive epistemic status therefore means that a given belief of a person fares favorably when analyzed and properly counts as knowledge for that person, whereas a negative epistemic status indicates that the belief in question cannot be said to be known by the person who believes it.

8. Craig, *Reasonable Faith*, 51. Although Craig subscribes to what he calls "classical apologetics," his basic understanding of the aim of apologetics is essentially the same as apologists of other methods. I address this further below.

means the activity of showing Christianity to be true to others requires logic and evidence. Craig elaborates:

> If, by proceeding on considerations that are common to both parties, such as sense perception, rational self-evidence, and common modes of reasoning, the Christian can show that his beliefs are true and those of his non-Christian friend are false, then he will have succeeded in showing that the Christian is in the better epistemic position for determining the truth in these matters. . . . The task of showing that Christianity is true involves the presentation of sound and persuasive arguments for Christian truth claims. Accordingly, we need to ask ourselves how it is that one proves something to be true. A statement or proposition is true if and only if it corresponds to reality—that is to say, reality is just as the statement says that it is. Thus, the statement "The cubs won the 1993 World Series" is true if and only if the Cubs won the 1993 World Series. In order to prove a proposition to be true, we present arguments and evidence which have that proposition as the conclusion. Such reasoning can be either deductive or inductive.[9]

The situation Craig describes, then, is something like this: Intelligent, informed Christians can *show* nonbelievers Christian theism is true—which genuine believers already *know* to be the case through the convicting work of the Holy Spirit—by presenting them with arguments and evidences that demonstrate the objective truth of the propositions (or statements) that express Christian beliefs. When these reasons for belief are combined with reasoned responses to challenges to Christian belief, they "show" or prove Christianity "is the most plausible worldview a sufficiently informed, normal adult can adopt."[10] Apologetic arguments and evidences are extremely important to Craig because they are precisely what the Holy Spirit needs in order "to draw unbelievers to a knowledge of God by removing their sinful resistance to the conclusion of our arguments."[11] Having

9. Ibid., 51–52.
10. Craig, "Classical Apologetics," 54.
11. Ibid., 54. While Craig does say in *Reasonable Faith*, 46, that the Holy Spirit does not need to rely on "arguments and evidence" to convince the unbeliever that Christianity is true, he later writes again that "the role of the Holy Spirit is to use our arguments and evidence to convince the unbeliever of the truth of Christianity" (56). My reading is that Craig believes that in genuine apologetic situations—that

hit upon this account of Christian faith and the role of apologetics, Craig has discovered a way of thinking about Christian faith that he finds at once intellectually and experientially satisfying.

Secular Apologetics

What first strikes me in Craig's account of apologetics is his story can be told only by someone thoroughly immersed in the perspective of modernity. If we attend closely to the deeper assumptions at work in Craig's account, we find Craig's experience nicely illustrates what Charles Taylor refers to as our modern "condition of secularity."[12] To say it briefly, this condition of secularity is what makes it possible for us—unlike our premodern predecessors—to imagine the world (and ourselves) in such a way that the existence of God, and a transcendent or "higher" realm that makes sense of our world, is optional. Belief in God is not at all intuitive in the modern condition of secularity, and any interpretation of our world or experience that includes God runs into constant challenges. For most of us, God's existence is, in fact, inherently dubious and anything but self-evident. We *require* arguments and evidence for belief in God, and, failing that, we at least need a very good explanation (an epistemology perhaps) of how it is that belief in God is reasonable and counts as knowledge for us.

Perhaps nothing has contributed more to this condition of secularity than the modern invention of the "public sphere" as one of the central features of modern society. Prior to modernity, people did not tend to think in clearly drawn lines between what was public and what was private in civil life, and there was no social space imagined in which individuals might exist in such a way that they are not at the same time acting, thinking, and speaking within both the political and religious spheres as well. Premodern societies, therefore, tend not to speak of the separation of church and state, because these institutions and the

---

is, when the unbeliever does not accept the straightforward proclamation of biblical truth—the Holy Spirit then needs our further witness of arguments, by which the Spirit may then convince the unbeliever of the objective truth of Christianity.

12. Charles Taylor, *A Secular Age* (Cambridge, MA: Belknap, 2007), 14–18.

social spheres they represent are understood to be expressions of the same underlying reality, which transcends human time and space (the hierarchy of being).[13] To be sure, priest and king play different roles in premodern societies and they have different functions relative to this transcendence, but it is not as if one can understand social order and its rulers apart from the religious beliefs and practices that substantially shape it and give it legitimacy. So when I am fully installed in a premodern way of thinking, I have immense difficulty thinking of myself apart from social *and* religious terms (if this is possible at all).[14] My entire identity is fixed by its coordinates in socioreligious reality and cannot be understood without reference to my place in society and to God (or the gods) and God's purposes. That is to say, the premodern world thought of social life not so much in terms of public and private, civil and religious, but more as a unity of these different elements.

So the modern public sphere is something different from anything else that precedes it, because it is imagined as a neutral, common space free and disengaged from either the political or religious sphere. It is envisioned as a kind of shared space in which people who never actually meet physically with each other nevertheless understand themselves to be engaged in discussion and capable of reaching a rational consensus.[15] This division of life into private and public is critical to the entire conception of modern life, as Taylor observes, because it enables modern societies to see themselves as capable of coming to agreement without having to appeal to political or religious authority. They imagine themselves to be engaged in "a discourse of reason *outside power*, which nevertheless is normative for power."[16] If we look at the impact of the modern public sphere on Christian belief,

13. Premodern social life is a form of embeddedness within *the cosmos itself*. There is a mystery or plenitude to the cosmos. It is *enchanted*, as Taylor puts it, and there are forces and spirits that influence and act on me that are beyond my control. See Charles Taylor, *Modern Social Imaginaries* (Durham, NC: Duke University Press, 2004), 51–56.

14. Ibid.

15. Ibid., 85.

16. Ibid., 91 (my emphasis). Thus, as Scott Baker pointed out to me, the crucial question asked by modern theorists of the public square is the question as to who is administering that neutrality, its norm, and its rules.

then we can discern at least two very important effects: (1) it now becomes possible to imagine that questions about religious beliefs—for example, belief in God's existence—can be settled objectively and neutrally, without appeal to sectarian interests; and (2) whatever beliefs about God (the gods, faith, etc.) I may hold, in modernity we may now suppose they are my private affair and of no concern to anyone else.

When Taylor describes the height of modernity—the Enlightenment—as "the Great Disembedding," he has in mind the net effect of the modern condition of secularity and the creation of the modern public square.[17] The process of Enlightenment brought about (or was itself brought about by) a massive shift in how individual and corporate identities are imagined by individuals in modern societies, together with the practices that give shape to their identities. To put a finer point on it, the shift to modernity uninstalls the premodern self from the hierarchical cosmos of harmonized meanings and corporate socioreligious identity in which everything is well-ordered and has its place and reality is fundamentally *enchanted*, even mysterious.[18] Instead, the modern person is embedded in a different kind of "social imaginary"[19] altogether—one in which disenchantment, reform, and personal religion all go together.[20] It is the kind of worldview that is virtually unable to appeal to anything beyond the physical universe to justify belief or rational argument, and that places the responsibility for justifying beliefs on the individuals who hold them.

So we can say the crisis of faith Craig describes appears to be generated by his embeddedness in a modern world insofar as it requires that God's existence is not intuitively plausible and that individuals are responsible to justify their beliefs rationally for themselves. The entire story of his intensely personal need to produce an apologetic for Christian faith that makes his personal experience intelligible in terms of "the demands of reason" signals that Craig's is a profoundly

17. Taylor, *A Secular Age*, 146.
18. Ibid., 26, explains, "The enchanted world in this sense is the world of spirits, demons, and moral forces which our ancestors lived in."
19. A "social imaginary" includes the complex and elusive set of values, background practices, and horizons of common expectations that shape our social identities. It is not, as Taylor explains, a set of ideas per se but rather what enables the practices of society by making them intelligible. *Modern Social Imaginaries*, 2.
20. Ibid., 50.

modern experience. And perhaps most important, Craig imagines that his apologetic arguments are normative to society but take place in a public sphere *outside* political or religious power. They are "neutral" means of establishing the rock-bottom truth about things regardless of one's vantage point or perspective. All things being equal (e.g., intelligence), the only hindrances to our understanding and beliefs are our evil intentions and the hardness of our hearts. And Craig imagines he is engaged in a public conversation in which rational consensus is not only possible but is absolutely vital to society and Christian faith. Craig is thoroughly disembedded from a premodern imaginary.

What also strikes me is that Craig's apologetic paradigm conceives of truth, reason, and faith solely in terms of the modern epistemological paradigm. Philosophical modernism and the Enlightenment is marked by an attempt to free human thought from its dependence on external sources—such as traditions, assumptions, or other authorities—for the grounds of belief.[21] This project is critical to secular modernity because it has stripped away from the premodern cosmos its implicit *raison d'etre*. As an oversimplification, we might say the premodern cosmos is an organized unity of beings arranged to reflect God (or the Good), who is the point of it all.[22] Things (and persons) are "good" in this world to the degree they reflect their proper relation to the Cause or Source of all Goodness. There is no substantial gap, then, between reality and being, God and the cosmos, even if there is a manifest distinction between the beings and the Being of it all. God and the world (with all its beings) come as a piece, and what makes them intelligible is the word (*logos*, reason) that shapes both

21. Compare the summary of "the modern Enlightenment doctrine of prejudice" elaborated by Hans-Georg Gadamer, which he boils down to this: "Have the courage to make use of your *own* understanding." *Truth and Method*, 2nd, rev. ed., trans. rev. Joel Weinsheimer and Donald G. Marshall (New York: Continuum, 2004), 271.

22. These are very broad brushstrokes here, and I am speaking directly of the dominant ethos in Western society. We must not lose sight of the fact that premodernity was not homogeneous. Here it is important to remember that conceptual categories of "modern," "premodern," and "postmodern" are themselves heuristic tools that once understood and used can be set aside. Cf. Myron B. Penner, "Christianity and the Postmodern Turn: Some Preliminary Considerations," in *Christianity and the Postmodern Turn: Six Views*, ed. Myron B. Penner (Grand Rapids: Brazos, 2005), 19.

minds and matter. Modern consciousness, however, conceives of the world as a machine, and it thinks of the human person (more or less) as a disembodied mind that is the free and unencumbered center of rational thought. We may describe this modern phenomenon as a shift from *logos* to logic—from an embodied rationality to a formal view of reason that is understood in technical and procedural terms.[23] The task of reason in modernity is principally epistemological: its function is to measure, categorize, and exercise intellectual mastery and control over an otherwise brute and irrational universe that does not necessarily have a purpose, a center, or even a unifying principle.[24] But reason is also the possession of *individuals*—not the universe— and is something each person has and must exercise.[25] The telling point of Craig's story in this regard is his admission that until he hit upon his "knowing" and "showing" distinction, the relationship between faith and reason vexed him. He was caught on the horns of a dilemma that left him in an untenable position for a modern thinker. On the one hand, his experience with Jesus was such that he could not deny it, and yet he had no theory (or evidence) that made it rational. His only way to pass through this dilemma unscathed was to articulate an epistemology that made his experience of God rationally defensible.

A final conspicuous feature of Craig's account of apologetics is that, contrary to how he seems to want to think about them, both knowing

23. I describe the shift from premodern to modern notions of human being in more detail in Myron B. Penner, "Christianity and the Postmodern Turn."
24. Cf. Barry Allen, *Truth in Philosophy* (Cambridge, MA: Harvard University Press, 1993), 19–20, and Calvin O. Schrag, *The Resources of Rationality: A Response to the Postmodern Challenge* (Bloomington, IN: Indiana University Press, 1992), 1, 17–18.
25. One may try to argue, as Douglas Groothuis attempts in "Postmodern Falla- cies: A Response to Merold Westphal," *Christian Century*, July 26, 2003, that such a description of modernism "may loosely fit Descartes, but few others," and charge postmodernists with attempting "to legitimize themselves by reacting to an overblown stereotype." But this response seems itself a bit of a caricature. Merold Westphal notes in "Postmodern Fallacies: Merold Westphal Replies," *Christian Century*, July 26, 2003, that at a minimum, modern philosophers from both the rationalist tradi- tions (Descartes, Leibniz, Spinoza) and empiricist traditions (Locke, Hume, J. S. Mill—and I would add Berkley), as well as the critical philosophy of the eighteenth and nineteenth centuries in Germany (Kant, Hegel) and the nineteenth and twentieth century positivists, fall under this description of modernity: "We are not talking about an 'overblown stereotype'"!

and showing for him are ways of describing how Christian belief is *rational* (in the modern sense). And this is due in no small part to his conviction that being a Christian amounts to giving intellectual assent to specific propositions.[26] Those who find them a useful part of a theory of language generally think of a proposition as whatever is expressed by a sentence. They are what makes it possible to say the same thing in different languages and help explain why many different sentences can say the same thing (i.e., they all repeat the same proposition in different modalities).[27] Since modernity has rejected the premodern idea that the universe is structured by an inherently rational principle, there has to be some way of connecting the human rational mind to the brute universe. Premodern thought is more inclined to understand the human mind as encountering or participating in the world directly, without anything mediating it.[28] This is possible, as we just saw, because the mind and reality are similarly structured by *logos*. But in modernity this tends to happen in the form of propositions that express "facts" of the universe, which are thought to be objective features of the universe. Once Craig and modern apologists accept the propositional nature of Christian revelation and truth, the way is open for them to insist Christian truths are "objective facts" that can (and must) be defended

26. See Craig, *Reasonable Faith, passim*, where he just assumes that to say Christianity is true is to speak of it in propositional terms. Craig, here, is only following the dominant trend in American evangelical theology of at least the ilk of Charles Hodge and Carl Henry, which emphasizes the propositional nature of Christian revelation. Cf. Carl F. H. Henry: "Christianity contends that revelational truth is intelligible, expressible in valid propositions, and universally communicable. Christianity does not profess to communicate a meaning that is significant only within a particular community or culture. It expects men of all cultures and nations to comprehend its claims about God and insists that men everywhere ought to acknowledge and appropriate them." *God, Revelation, and Authority*, vol. 1 (Waco: Word, 1976), 126.

27. J. P. Moreland offers a useful summary, saying that "a proposition (1) is not located in space or time; (2) is not identical to the linguistic entities that may be used to express it; (3) is not sense perceptible; (4) is such that the same proposition may be in more than one mind at once; (5) need not be grasped by any (at least finite) person to exist and be what it is; (6) may itself be an object of thought when, for example, one is thinking about the content of one's own thought processes; (7) is in no sense a physical entity." "Truth, Contemporary Philosophy, and the Postmodern Turn," *Journal of the Evangelical Theological Society* 48 (2005): 84.

28. Cf. Charles Taylor, *Philosophical Arguments* (Cambridge, MA: Harvard University Press, 1995), 3; and Fergus Kerr, *After Aquinas: Versions of Thomism* (Oxford: Blackwell, 2002), 28–30.

with arguments and evidences that are objectively true, universally accessible, and free from bias or partisanship.

In the modern philosophical paradigm, then, reason forms what I will call the "objective-universal-neutral complex" (OUNCE). I use this rather awkward language to signal that the view of reason that emerges in the modern public sphere is one that is re-construed as a distinctly human quality—or at least the quality of "mind" (vesus matter). No longer is reason thought of as the structuring feature of the world external to the human mind, as in the premodern view. Instead, reason is internal to (and possessed only by) human beings in a way that is universal, ob-jective, and neutral. Because of this, any rational person may judge the worthiness of any other belief. As *universal*, every reasonable human being possesses the ability to *access* the rational grounds of belief; as *objective*, every reasonable person possesses the ability to *assess* the grounds for belief; and as *neutral*, every reasonable person possesses the *authority* to judge the merits of any belief. It is this combination which, in the end, forms an imperative that every person *must* justify each and every belief—and, I should add, has a moral duty to accept only those beliefs genuinely known.[29] So the move to propositions as the main bearers of Christian truth and revelation is important to Craig and modern apologists—and important for them *to defend*—because propositions are exactly the kinds of entities that must exist if one is to communicate and defend truths according to the demands of OUNCE.[30]

---

29. Craig's insistence on the internal testimony of the Holy Spirit notwithstand-ing (along with the contention of Reformed Epistemology that a person may be well within epistemic rights to believe in God even in the absence of any evidence or arguments to support it), the critical question to ask of Craig and our Reformed epistemologists is, What happens when *no one* in the epistemic community is able to articulate this epistemological thesis and make it intelligible? What is the status of belief in God in *these* circumstances? And how is the apologetic agenda affected by this? Presumably, the finely nuanced and well-articulated theories of Craig and the Reformed epistemologists are symptoms of this facet of the modern apologetic paradigm. (Why do they feel the need to formulate them?) Furthermore, in Craig's case of the internal testimony of the Holy Spirit, the person is, in fact, convinced of the epistemic appropriateness of belief (supernaturally) anyway, and proceeds with faith on that basis.

30. This is also why modern apologists defend a modern version of the corre-spondence theory of truth, which views truth as the correspondence between reality and our words by means of propositions. For one of the more extensive statements of this position within the modern apologetic paradigm, see chapter 3, "The Biblical

It is not difficult to see how the shift to modernity, then, also entails
a new—and diminished—status for Christian thought. In the sixteenth
century, for example, just prior to modernity, Christian belief was
virtually taken for granted in the West.[31] Christian faith had never
purported to be objective or neutral or universal in the sense that
modernity defines these, and it had operated for centuries embedded
within a premodern worldview, along with premodern sources of belief
and rationality. Modern challenges to Christian faith, however, attack
the very sources of belief, not just the content of Christian doctrine.
Objections to faith are now no longer of the sort that question whether
a given belief is true, but much more substantially concern how anyone
could believe Christian doctrine at all, given the basis on which it is
traditionally believed (e.g., church tradition and Scripture). Issues
such as the epistemological reliability of Scripture, the intellectual
coherence of theism or miracles, the historicity of the resurrection of
Jesus, and so on, take center stage in modern discussions of Christian
faith. What is more, given the ethos of modernity, the cultural pres-
sure to provide substantial answers to these questions is enormous.

It is just this context that gives rise to modern apologetics of
the sort engaged in by Craig. Christian apologists—particularly
Protestants—respond to modern challenges to Christianity in a variety of ways but generally fall into two basic types of theological
response: either one accepts that orthodoxy needs to be updated
and therefore tries to rehabilitate Christian doctrine and show its
continuing relevance and explanatory power; or one attempts to
meet the Enlightenment challenges head-on by demonstrating that
orthodox Christian belief is compatible with the new science and
the modern way of thinking about the world. The first theological
response is what we often refer to as the "liberal" theological project
and produces an "apologetic theology" that accommodates Christian
belief to modern science and culture, adjusting traditional orthodoxy
according to the results of rational investigation. The second theological response is the one in which Craig is interested and that we

View of Truth," in Douglas Groothuis, *Truth Decay: Defending Christianity Against
the Challenges of Postmodernity* (Downers Grove, IL: InterVarsity, 2002), 60–82.

31. The most thorough treatment of this phenomenon is Charles Taylor's impressive work *A Secular Age.*

generally associate with "conservative" theology. It uses apologetics defensively to preserve the reasonability (OUNCE) of more traditional Christian belief, particularly defending the Bible as an epistemically reliable source of beliefs.[32] Modern theology, then, splits along liberal and conservative lines, depending on the response to the diminished status of Christian belief. Methodologically, the difference between them concerns their understandings of the nature and role of revelation in Christian belief. The key, though, is that both the liberal and conservative apologetic projects imagine the world in roughly the same modern way—so that the Christian worldview is justified according to the same concept of reason, albeit with opposing approaches and conclusions.[33]

The modern conflict between liberal and conservative Christianity plays a critical part in Craig's story about coming to his apologetic method. When Craig disparages the "theological rationalism" of the Christian college he attended, he quite clearly means they are of the liberal bent, willing to revise Christian belief according to the dictates of modern reason and culture. The method Craig hits upon, however, is to his mind free from this rationalism because it acknowledges a rather traditional role for the Holy Spirit and supernatural revelation in the epistemic process. What Craig fails to see, however, is that his (conservative) agenda is defined just as much by modernity as the "theological rationalism" he opposes— and is every bit as complicit with its assumptions. Of course, there are substantial and important differences between conservative and liberal theologies, but their disagreements belie a common commitment to the modern paradigm.[34]

Since there are a variety of avowed apologetic styles and methods used by Christian apologists, I must be careful not to paint them all with the same brush. According to Steven Cowan's classification,

32. Ironically, conservatives and liberals alike end up revising Christian faith quite dramatically.

33. Cf. Stanley J. Grenz and John R. Franke, *Beyond Foundationalism: Shaping Theology in a Postmodern Context* (Louisville: Westminster John Knox, 2001), 30–37.

34. Despite the fact that my primary concern in this book is with the more conservative apologetic project of the sort Craig engages, my critique extends to modern liberal apologetic theology as well.

there are five distinct apologetic methods.[35] The first is Craig's "two-step" Classical Method, which we have already given a cursory look. As Craig develops this method, it begins with natural theology to establish theism (belief in the existence of a personal, all-powerful, all-knowing, and good God who created and sustains the universe) as the correct worldview and then moves from theism to evidences for the Christian God. The second method, the Evidential Method, is a "one-step" method that argues for Christian beliefs directly from evidences, without bothering first to argue for the credibility of a theistic worldview. Third, the Cumulative Case Method models its argument for Christian rational superiority after a lawyer's brief and argues that the Christian worldview has more overall explanatory power than alternative hypotheses. Fourth, the Presuppositional Method presupposes the truth of Christianity as the starting point for apologetic argument and then argues "transcendentally"[36] that all meaning and thought logically presupposes the God of the Christian Scriptures. And finally, the Reformed Epistemology Method begins with a sophisticated analytic epistemology built around the proposition that belief in God does not need argument or evidence to be rational—instead, belief in God is taken as a "properly basic" item of knowledge, in a similar move to Craig's epistemology of knowing God's existence.

The point, however, is that while these various apologists may disagree as to *how* one makes the case for Christianity or what the

---

35. Steven B. Cowan, introduction to *Five Views on Apologetics*, ed. Steven B. Cowan (Grand Rapids: Zondervan, 2000), 7–20. I should note that David Clark's proposal in *Dialogical Apologetics: A Person-Centered Approach* is a fascinating one that attempts to position itself as a distinct innovation on the five apologetic types discussed in Cowan's *Five Views on Apologetics*. Clark's "dialogical apologetics" reconceives apologetics by adding the personal dimension to the rational side of traditional apologetics. "Traditionally," Clark argues, "*apologetics* has been defined as the *art of the reasoned defense of the Christian faith.*" Clark's new approach, however, defines apologetics as "the art of the reasoned defense of the Christian faith *in the context of personal dialogue*" (Grand Rapids: Baker, 1993), 114. As will become obvious, I find this attention to the person in dialogue extremely significant and important. Clark's proposal, though much more in line with mine here, falls (just) short of being radical enough and remains entrenched in the modern epistemological paradigm.

36. A transcendental argument is a deductive argument for the necessary conditions of a possibility. In this case, presuppositional apologists argue that God is a necessary condition for the possibility of any human knowledge at all.

exact relationship between faith and reason is, they nonetheless agree with Craig regarding the *central goal* of apologetics, which is *to make Christian beliefs rationally warranted (or justified)* for both the believer and the unbeliever.[37] And if this does not happen—or worse, if it *cannot* happen—then, according to each of the apologetic methods just described, Christian belief is implausible and ought not to be taken seriously. So the shared aim of all the varieties of modern apologetics is to make Christian belief plausible in this modern situation in which belief in God is not at all obvious or intuitive. To accomplish this, modern apologists use arguments, evidence, or a philosophical account of the Christian worldview that conforms to OUNCE. The aim of modern apologetics, in other words, is thoroughly epistemological in the modern sense. What is essential to being a Christian is an objective event: the cognitive acceptance (belief) of specific propositions (doctrines). And because Christianity is essentially objective in this way (propositionally), it can (and must) have an objective basis or rational foundation that complies with OUNCE.

The degree to which contemporary apologetics (and apologists) share this aim of modern thought and attempt to make Christian beliefs rationally warranted (or justified) according to the modern project and in terms of OUNCE, is the same degree to which they are a version of *secular apologetics*. I use the term "secular apologetics" for this kind of project because this sort of apologetics does not need to appeal to a higher transcendent ground for Christian truths and instead justifies them exclusively in immanent human reason. This is, in other words, exactly the kind of reason-giving practice one would expect to find in the modern secular condition.

37. James K. A. Smith argues that insofar as presuppositional apologetics recognizes the role played by presuppositions in both what counts as true and what is recognized as true, it is postmodern. *Who's Afraid of Postmodernism? Taking Derrida, Lyotard, and Foucault to Church* (Grand Rapids: Baker Academic, 2006), 28. Smith is particularly keen to follow the strategy of apologist Francis Schaeffer (20). While the acknowledgment of the crucial role of presuppositions makes it *closer* to a postmodern view of the kind I am describing here, I cannot quite agree that it *is* postmodern as I use the term. By my account, presuppositional apologetics—particularly Francis Schaeffer's—is thoroughly modern so far as it continues the modern preoccupation with epistemology. See John Frame, "Presuppositional Apologetics," in Cowan, *Five Views on Apologetics*, especially 208–14. Cf. Francis A. Schaeffer, *Escape From Reason* (Downers Grove, IL: InterVarsity, 1968), 28–29.

Apologies to Postmodernism

Perhaps nowhere are the deep commitments of contemporary apologetics to the modern paradigm more obvious than when it is responding to the perceived threats of postmodernism. In this regard, modern apologists serve to reinforce the contention of postmodern theorist Jean-François Lyotard that modernity is the attempt to overcome postmodernity.[38] Modern apologists have a remarkable and pronounced tendency to treat postmodernism as a set of beliefs, tenets, or propositions that are meant to provide some sort of epistemological foundation, justification, or set of arguments for how one ought to understand the world.[39] And, when they engage postmodernity, they often assume one may do so rather straightforwardly using the same assumptions, techniques, and modes of discourse that emerge from the modern discourse on Christian faith.[40] They attempt to understand

38. Jean-François Lyotard, *The Postmodern Condition: A Report on Knowledge*, trans. Geoff Bennington and Brian Massumi (Minneapolis: University of Minnesota, 1984), 79. See Penner, "Christianity and the Postmodern Turn," 19, for a brief discussion of this.

39. James K. A. Smith discusses this same phenomenon in relation to one (albeit important) segment of the contemporary apologetic community. "Who's Afraid of Postmodernism? A Response to the Biola School," in *Christianity and the Postmodern Turn*, 215–28.

40. For example, William Lane Craig seems to define postmodernism as a thesis about diversity and irreducible plurality and, in particular, as adhering to the doctrine of "universal salvation." "Politically Incorrect Salvation," in *Christian Apologetics in the Postmodern World*, ed. Timothy R. Phillips and Dennis Okholm (Downers Grove, IL: InterVarsity, 1995), 75, 97. See also William Lane Craig, *Reasonable Faith*, where he claims that "the idea that we live in a postmodern culture is a myth" and that "a postmodern culture is an impossibility" because "postmodernists reject the traditional canons of logic, rationality, and truth" (18). For more examples of this trend in Christian apologetics, see Groothuis, *Truth Decay*, 32–59; Phillip E. Johnson, *Reason in the Balance: The Case Against Naturalism in Science, Law, and Education* (Downers Grove, IL: InterVarsity, 1995); Millard J. Erickson, *Truth or Consequences: The Perils and Promises of Postmodernism* (Downers Grove, IL: InterVarsity, 2001); Moreland, "Truth, Contemporary Philosophy, and the Postmodern Turn," 77–88; R. Douglas Geivett, "Is God a Story? Postmodernity and the Task of Theology," in Myron B. Penner, *Christianity and the Postmodern Turn: Six Views* (Grand Rapids: Brazos, 2005), 37–52; and R. Scott Smith, "Christian Postmodernism and the Linguistic Turn," in Penner, *Christianity and the Postmodern Turn*, 53–70. We see a much more nuanced version of this approach in Timothy R. Phillips's and Dennis Okholm's introduction to *Christian Apologetics in the Postmodern World*, 13, where they define postmodernism in terms of "two constitutive elements"—the rejection

postmodernism as something primarily conceptual—and therefore
without a lived context—rather than in terms of its overall *ethos*.
And they do so with no regard to the concerns and circumstances
in which postmodern discourse emerges. The typical strategy for
modern apologists in responding to postmodern disbelief in God is
to begin by defending the modern philosophical move to understand
truth, reason, belief, and so on in terms of OUNCE as the correct approach. It then goes on to show how postmodernism is a rejection of
all this. The obvious conclusion is then drawn that postmodernism is
rationally and morally objectionable, silly, misguided, and something
no believer in Jesus could ever seriously consider.

Craig's colleague and fellow apologist J. P. Moreland falls squarely
into this pattern in his attempt to refute postmodernism.[41] Moreland
defines postmodernism as a species of *antirealism*—the denial of an
external reality—as well as advancing specific philosophical theses
and doctrines such as Descartes's theory of ideas. Despite his promis-
ing recognition that "postmodernism is a loose coalition of diverse
thinkers" and that "it is difficult to characterize postmodernism in
a way that would be fair to this diversity," he nevertheless wants to
understand postmodernism as a philosophical *position*—an *epistemological* position, to be precise.[42] According to Moreland, "postmodernism is primarily a reinterpretation of what knowledge is and
what counts as knowledge." Broadly speaking, "it represents a form
of cultural relativism" and "on a postmodernist view, there is no
such thing as objective reality, truth, value, reason, and so forth."[43] To
Moreland's mind, postmodern thought starts and ends in suspicion
and eventually emerges as a form of nihilism that denies meaning,

---

of oppressive "totalizing metanarratives" and "the relativism of Richard Rorty and
Stanley Fish." Interestingly, many of the other contributors to *Christian Apologetics
in the Postmodern World* do not take the approach to postmodernism I am attributing
to the modern apologetic paradigm.

41. See especially Moreland, "Truth, Contemporary Philosophy, and the Postmodern Turn."

42. Moreland, "Truth, Contemporary Philosophy, and the Postmodern Turn,"
79. Examples of this approach can be multiplied almost *ad infinitum*, but compare
another of Moreland's colleagues, Douglas Geivett, for a particularly pronounced
exhibition of this tendency ("Is God a Story," 37–52). James K. A. Smith responds to
Geivett in "Who's Afraid of Postmodernism? A Response to the Biola School," 216–18.

43. Moreland, "Truth, Contemporary Philosophy, and the Postmodern Turn," 79.

truth, knowledge, and value. All of this paves the way for Moreland to draw his conclusion that Christian intellectuals have the moral and spiritual responsibility to defend not just the truths of the Christian faith but also the very philosophical systems and concepts that make it possible to assert them as knowledge (according to modern criteria).[44] Postmodernism, Moreland concludes, is "immoral and cowardly" and a form of intellectual "pacifism" that lacks the courage to fight for the truth.[45] Instead of fighting the good apologetic fight for truth, knowledge, and the Christian way, it "recommends playing backgammon while the barbarians are at the gate."[46] Moreland therefore deems postmodernism antithetical to the gospel and believes Christian apologists must do all they can to defend the faith against it.

As I stated in the introduction, my main concern in this book is not to refute or rebut arguments like Moreland's—or those of any other apologists—but to tell a different story than they do.[47] I assume postmodernism as a starting point in order to see how the apologetic paradigm looks from that perspective, and I view postmodernism as a philosophical *movement*, with a cluster of philosophical positions (including an overall orientation to epistemic questions) that characterizes that movement, rather than as a philosophical *position* per se.[48] From this perspective, postmodernism is more a discursive event that materializes in the social and cultural conditions of late modernity. It is what comes after modernity. It is the attempt to think or theorize in conditions after, beyond, or outside of modernity. Postmodernism is therefore a *condition*—or, if you will, a set of dispositions or a *Zeitgeist*—and as such is simply not reducible to a set of philosophical propositions or doctrines about epistemology or anything else. It is true that postmodern perspectives usually understand human

44. Ibid., 87.
45. Ibid., 77.
46. Ibid., 88.
47. I have engaged Moreland's arguments against postmodernism in detail in "Cartesian Anxiety, Perspectivalism, and Truth: A Response to J. P. Moreland," *Philosophia Christi* 8, no. 1 (2006), 85–98.
48. That is, I try to follow Steven Connor's advice and "instead of asking, what is postmodern? . . . ask, where, how and why does the discourse of postmodernism flourish?, what is at stake in its debates?, who [sic] do they address and how?" *Postmodernist Culture: An Introduction to the Theories of the Contemporary* (Oxford: Basil Blackwell, 1989), 10.

consciousness and rationality as the product of the cultural, social, linguistic, psychological, and other historical forces at work in a person's concrete situation. But, as I see it, the postmodern ethos may *begin* with the moment of suspicion—particularly about how beliefs are justified in modernity—but it does not necessarily *end* in suspicion.

This being the case, it may just be possible after all to speak about Christian truth after modernity. If postmodern thought does not merely push the negative aspects of modernism to their ultimate nihilistic, skeptical conclusions, then adopting its vantage point may not be tantamount to selling the proverbial farm.[49] For my part, I believe postmodernism functions as a genuine critique of modernity and its atheistic impulses. This means that postmodernism has a relative value to Christians who are trying to think in different categories than the inherited modern values and assumptions that shape our culture. That is the task I have set for myself here in this book; only, if this is to be done, it cannot be performed in the same terms and under the same assumptions as in modernity. Such an account will have to look different, but I should think that does not thereby make it stupid, silly, immoral, or cowardly.

The breakdown in modern apologetic treatments of postmodernism like Moreland's is that postmodernism is examined from the perspective of OUNCE. Of course, one may get a fairly good idea of how postmodernism looks through *modernist* eyes this way, but it is by no means the only or best way to understand postmodernism—and it certainly does not address how postmodernists think about themselves. There is, therefore, a kind of intellectual astigmatism or blind spot produced by the perspective adopted by modern apologists, which enables them to treat postmodernism and modernism as similar types of philosophical positions. The ironic result is that modern apologists, for the most part, cannot see their own complicity with modernity—or, if they do, they associate themselves with only those parts of modernity that reinforce their assumptions about reason and faith.

Douglas Groothuis also bears out this conclusion as he attempts to define both modernism and postmodernism as "united in their

49. As a matter of fact, as we shall see later, I believe the shoe is on the other foot. It is *modern apologetics* that is in danger of collapsing under the unbearable lightness of modern nihilism.

philosophical naturalism."[50] Likewise, Phillip Johnson wants to identify modernity strictly with both naturalism and liberal rationalism so he can contrast modernism with his understanding of Christianity.[51] As it is quite apparent that Groothuis's and Johnson's descriptions of naturalism and liberal rationalism are *not* compatible with Christianity, they assume it also must be fairly clear that their views are not *modern* either. The thing to notice here is *all* worldviews are approached this way by modern apologetics—as if they were philosophical positions and propositions that are more or less disembodied and disconnected from the practices and practical concerns of everyday life. This includes the conceptual categories of premodernism, postmodernism, and even modernism itself. This kind of strategy makes it easy for modern apologists like Moreland, Groothuis, and Johnson to dismiss postmodernism and its challenge to the modern philosophical paradigm while at the same time remaining oblivious to the degree to which they share its deep commitments—such as OUNCE.

Incidentally, this modern approach to other worldviews is also what enables contemporary apologists to think of premodern believers as *theists* instead of Christians (or Muslims or Jews). As a concept, theism more or less refers to a minimal belief in an all-knowing, all-powerful, supremely good God who created and sustains the universe. The difficulty, of course, is no one actually *practices* theism. It is something of a modern intellectual fiction—perhaps useful in its own way—invented in order to facilitate the rational investigation of religion. Actual believers in the so-called theistic religions are members of historically situated worshipping communities that engage in specific practices and have beliefs—about God, the world, the nature of faith, etc.—that are a crucial part of making life and their world intelligible. God has a name—*Allah* or *Yahweh* or *Father–Son–Holy Spirit*—not a set of attributes, and a history, not a disembodied voice. And it is

50. Groothuis, *Truth Decay*, 38. Carl Raschke has mounted a scathing, and to my mind crushing, rebuttal to Groothuis and his sort of "response" to postmodernism in Carl Raschke, *The Next Reformation: Why Evangelicals Must Embrace Postmodernity* (Grand Rapids: Baker Academic, 2004), 11–33. My analysis here is complementary to Raschke's, only my focus is not on defending postmodernism per se. I am only pointing out a few of the internal problems with the modern apologetic responses to postmodernity.

51. Johnson, *Reason in the Balance*, 42.

in *these* concrete contexts that they may believe in a God who meets the minimum conditions to qualify as "theistic." But no one in these communities believes in their God in such a way as to think that the minimalistic account of the God of theism is a sufficient description of whom they worship. Their concept of God is a rich and full one that cannot be collapsed into the category of "theism."

What I find particularly concerning about Moreland's response to postmodernism—and Groothuis's and Johnson's—is what is defended in this apologetic effort is *not* the gospel or even an aspect of Christian doctrine but what amounts to the modern conception of reason (OUNCE) and modern philosophy in general. Craig, in fact, identifies the core of the Christian message so closely with modernism that he believes postmodern critiques of modernity are themselves a ploy of Satan to deceive people "into voluntarily laying aside our best weapons of logic and evidence," thereby assuring that Christianity will not achieve epistemic dominance in our culture.[52] I discuss this more in chapter 2, but it is interesting to observe here that Craig's version of modern apologetics is not only explicit about adopting a modern view of reason but also unequivocal about maintaining its rather overt ideological dimension. All of this supports Jonathan Wilson's contention that the overarching characteristic of the church's Enlightenment project can be summarized as "the attempt to commend the Gospel on grounds that have nothing to do with the Gospel itself."[53] What is at the bottom of our Christian belief, for modern apologists, is *not* a set of practices—a way of life, a confession, etc.—but a set of propositional asseverations that can be epistemically justified. And *that* is what it means for them to have faith. It is little wonder that postmodernism is, as Lyotard reminds us, such a threat to modern apologists that they must do all they can to defend against it.

Apologetic Amnesia

There is a definite missing-the-forest-for-the-trees phenomenon at work here. Contemporary apologists are prone to confuse the postmodern

52. Craig, *Reasonable Faith*, 18–19.
53. Wilson, *Living in a Fragmented Age*, 29.

viewpoint for modernism. The critical amnesia of apologists like Moreland makes it very difficult for them to see how their apologetic paradigm is *itself* a product of modernity. But modern apologists also tend to have the same shortsightedness in regard to premodernity. It is common for them to employ the arguments and strategies of premodern apologists as if there is no philosophical or social context that supervenes on either their concepts and arguments or those of their forbears. What we often find is that the natural theology of premodern Christian thought is appropriated in the modern context as offering arguments that conform to the objectives of OUNCE.

We can trace, as just one example, the way in which St. Thomas Aquinas's often disputed "Five Ways" of knowing God's existence (so-called natural theology) have come to take on quite a different meaning in Craig's modern "classical apologetics." Craig (and other contemporary apologists) seems to invoke Thomas's natural theology without paying much attention to the theological (and what is the same to Thomas, philosophical) assumptions that underlie them— or making even a passing reference to the premodern context that informs Aquinas's thought.[54] For instance, Craig argues that natural theology is entirely focused on presenting "arguments and evidence in support of theism independent of divine authoritative revelation."[55] But it is not at all incidental that Thomas formulates his "natural theology" in the theoretical context of the rest of his theology, which presupposes a certain understanding of the structure of reality (or metaphysics) and assumes the existence of God as creator and the self-diffusive Good throughout creation. For Thomas—as for premoderns in general—human reason functions in conformity to the *logos* of the universe and does not and *could not* operate under the constraints of OUNCE. So when premodern Christian thinkers engage natural theology, their appeal is always situated within a specific set of practices of the community of faith—the life of devotion and prayer that gives their worldview its context and meaning.[56] The motivation,

54. See Fergus Kerr, "Ways of Reading The Five Ways," in *After Aquinas*, 52–72. Charles Taylor also makes reference to this same phenomenon in *A Secular Age*, 294–95.
55. Craig, *Reasonable Faith*, 24.
56. This is obvious in the case of St. Anselm of Canterbury's so-called ontological argument for God's existence, which is set explicitly within a prayer. See Anselm,

then, for undertaking natural theology is primarily *dogmatic*, not *apologetic* in the modern sense.[57]

Unlike Craig's classical apologetics,[58] when Thomas talks about "knowing," "reason," or "truth"—or any other theoretical entity—he simply does not understand these concepts in the terms spelled out by the modern paradigm. To begin with, he does not find himself in the modern condition of secularity and does not imagine himself to be engaged in an objective, dispassionate discourse outside of political power. His apologetic strategy is also not based on the assumption that the universe is impersonal or that the reasons we have for belief in God can be held rationally apart from a worldview that has minimally theistic commitments. That this realization eludes Craig and most other Christian apologists is a function of the self-forgetfulness generated by their commitment to the modern epistemological paradigm (OUNCE) and the modern practices that disengage self and reason from the universe.

My contention here, then, is that contemporary apologetic discourse comes directly out of the modern epistemic paradigm and its particular way of understanding the world, its method of addressing the problems and questions that emerge in the modern world, as well as the anxieties that make these questions appear both urgent and natural and the products of rational progress. In stark contrast to the church's earliest apologists, a kind of *apologetic positivism* emerges in modern Christian thought, according to which Christian beliefs must be demonstrably rational to be accepted.[59] In effect, this positivism becomes the default posture of modern Christian thought and the means to securing truthful Christian speech. This is true for

Proslogion: With Replies to Gaunilo, trans. Thomas Williams (Indianapolis: Hackett, 1995, 2001). See also Marilyn McCord Adams, "Praying the Proslogion," in *The Rationality of Belief and the Plurality of Faith*, ed. Thomas Senor (Ithaca, NY: Cornell University Press, 1995), 13–39.

57. Cf. Alastair E. McGrath, *The Order of Things: Explorations in Scientific Theology* (Oxford: Blackwell, 2006), 72–73.

58. See the discussion of Thomas in Craig, *Reasonable Faith*, 32–33, and 97–98.

59. I am stretching (and changing) the meaning of positivism, which was an early-twentieth-century movement that limited genuine knowledge to that which is derived from sense experience and positively verified as such. Here I want to cash in on the reductionism at play in this concept of knowledge as well as its emphasis on positive verification as the prerequisite for appropriate belief.

both sides of the so-called liberal/conservative divide in Christian theology, though it is manifested differently for each. Liberal apologetic positivism tends toward a reductionism that shrinks the tenets of Christian faith in accordance with that which is apologetically verifiable. Conservative apologetic positivism results in fixation on the rational demonstrability of the "fundamentals" of Christian faith. So the only substantial difference between the two sides concerns how much orthodox doctrine they think is rationally supportable.

It is as if Christians have a moral duty to believe only those aspects of Christian doctrine that have a sufficient apologetic basis.[60] This indicates a significant shift in the basis for Christian belief, why it is to be believed, and how it should be expressed. The earliest Christian apologists saw theology not just as a rational principle that governs the cognitive content of our beliefs but as intimately connected to a wider way of living and being together that embodies the truth of the gospel.[61] However, in order to fend off modern attacks and establish itself as a legitimate branch of knowledge, modern theology focuses on articulating the contours of the Christian worldview in a coherent system that establishes Christian doctrine as a rational body of knowledge. The truth of the gospel is made evident by its conformity to modern standards of rationality. Modern Christians have a difficult time understanding how it could be any other way. Modern science supplies us with the most rigorous and exact standards for determining truth, and if Christianity really is the truth, modern apologetics will need to apply those standards to Christian belief and demonstrate how Christian belief passes muster.

For all intents and purposes, then, the modern apologetic paradigm is deeply embedded in the epistemological paradigm of modernity—it shares its goals, its questions, its basic methods, and, even more important, its practices. That is to say, the Christian apologetic paradigm

60. I mean this to be a play on the now infamous declaration of seventeenth-century British mathematician and philosopher William K. Clifford regarding the epistemic duties of all rational people: "It is wrong always, everywhere and for any person to believe anything upon insufficient evidence." "The Ethics of Belief," in *The Rationality of Christian Belief,* ed. George A. Mavrodes (Englewood Cliffs, NJ: Prentice-Hall, 1970), 152–60.

61. Cf. Brad J. Kallenberg, *Ethics as Grammar: Changing the Postmodern Subject* (Notre Dame, IN: University of Notre Dame Press, 2001), 158.

shares the philosophical horizon of modernity and is thoroughly immersed in its ethos. This ethos of modernity is defined by secularity, in which the existence of God is not intuitively plausible and the reasons we have for believing in God—or anything else—must be objective, universal, and neutral. In fact, in the modern imagination, justifying our beliefs in this way is the fundamental philosophical concern. The driving need to prove the scientific viability of Christian beliefs, the rational superiority of the Christian worldview, or the so-called case for Christianity signals an underlying preoccupation with mastery and control through rational dominance and a conviction that modern systematic theology done well yields the most enlightened form of the Christian faith. Despite what Christian apologists may tell themselves and others about how much they oppose modern philosophical assumptions or the dominant views of modernity, they nevertheless are in fundamental agreement with modern thinkers about which questions are the important ones, how those questions need to be answered, and why they need answering.[62]

In the next chapter I look at some further implications of the modern secular condition and how it shows up in the modern apologetic paradigm.

62. Cf. Michael Buckley, SJ, *At the Origins of Modern Atheism* (New Haven: Yale University Press, 1987).

2

Apologetics, Suspicion, and Faith

Good philosophy must exist, if for no other reason, because bad philosophy must be answered.

C. S. Lewis

The fundamentalist is like the kind of neurotic who can't
trust that he is loved, but in infantile spirit demands some
irrefragable proof of the fact.

Slavoj Žižek

One of the popular forms of modern apologetic discourse is
the academic debate. My initiation into apologetic debates
happened during my first year at university. A Christian apologist,
who was touring university campuses, was invited by my university's
chapter of Inter-Varsity Christian Fellowship (IVCF) to debate the
resident atheist in our philosophy department. This particular atheist professor had banished belief in God as a rational thought from
countless freshman philosophy students' minds and had planted seeds
of doubt in the hearts of many a fervent member of our IVCF group.
Just as we saw William Lane Craig confess in the previous chapter,

47

there was a high level of anxiety in our IVCF chapter over the relationship between the claims of our Christian faith and the standards
of reasonability we were being taught at university.

So a good number of us were elated to learn that an expert in
Christian apologetics was coming who would definitively prove to
everyone at our university that belief in God is rationally superior to
atheism—and that we Christians are not as naive and asinine as we
are often made out to be. To make the conclusion unambiguous, the
audience would be polled to determine the winner. This was billed by
us in IVCF as an unparalleled witnessing opportunity, and we urged
our members to invite at least one friend. In the end, the Christian
apologist was the winner with about 80 percent of the popular vote.
The result was decisive, we felt, and it was regarded as a triumph for
the cause of Christ. I remember being a little uneasy, though, as I
looked around the room and noted that about 80 percent of people
in the room were people I knew from IVCF (or their guests).

This experience illustrates a feature of the modern apologetic paradigm that I find particularly telling. Note how the apologist debater
functions something like an expert witness who is uniquely gifted
and highly trained—and therefore especially qualified—to articulate
and defend Christian truth in a way the rest of us cannot. Objections
to Christian faith in modernity come from the intelligentsia—from
the highly sophisticated and intellectually rigorous modern scientific
worldview. As the challenge is for Christians to articulate the epistemological warrant or justification for their beliefs in terms that are
objective, universal, and neutral, the average Christian in the pew
may not possess the intellectual qualifications or have the requisite
training to defend the faith. It is difficult, often, to even *understand*
the objections to faith, let alone know how to respond to them.
When, for example, Stephen Hawking and Leonard Mlodinow tell
us "M-theory is the only model that has all the properties we think
the final theory [i.e., 'the ultimate theory of everything'] ought to
have," and M-theory in turn answers all the questions of creation so
belief in God is irrelevant, how many of us, really, are in a position
to disagree (or agree, for that matter)? I for one would have to study
up quite a lot on my physics to even understand M-theory before

being able to understand this claim, let alone determine its accuracy.[1] In short, we *need* experts for this kind of witness.

I want to explore this modern apologetic culture of experts further in this chapter, because I think it tells us something very important about the modern condition of secularity and the concept of reason that is adopted by modern apologetics. I suggest modern Christian apologetics subtly undermines the very gospel it seeks to defend and does not offer us a good alternative to the skepticism and ultimate meaninglessness of the modern secular condition.

Of Geniuses and Apostles

In his autopsy of modern apologetics, Kierkegaard addresses what I call the modern secular condition by drawing a very careful distinction between a genius and an apostle.[2] For Kierkegaard, a genius is something like our concept of an "expert."[3] According to Kierkegaard, genius becomes the default authority for our beliefs and practices in modernity. A genius is the highest person on the intellectual totem pole, the first in our pecking order of whom to believe. If I want to know if I should accept a given belief or follow a certain practice, I either establish its reasonableness for myself (if I am capable of doing so) or simply trace back to the source of the claim or action under consideration to determine whether those who recommend it are experts in their field. Geniuses (or experts) are able to provide this kind of epistemic assurance for us because they are "leaders in their field"—they know

1. Stephen Hawking and Leonard Mlodinow, *The Grand Design* (New York: Bantam Books, 2010), 8. Of course, I can read their book and perhaps even understand their explanation of M-theory in it, along with their argument, but I still only understand M-theory through their explanation of it and I just have to take their word for it.
2. See his essay "On the Difference Between a Genius and an Apostle," in the appendix of Søren Kierkegaard, *The Book on Adler*, ed. and trans. Howard V. Hong and Edna H. Hong (Princeton: Princeton University Press, 2009).
3. There is, however, a marked contrast between Kierkegaard's concept of a genius and our concept of an expert insofar as a genius is always defined over against others ("the crowd"). Another of the major dissimilarities between the Kierkegaardian concept of a genius and our concept of an expert is that for us an expert is part of a community of mutually recognized "experts" who act as the authorities for a particular field of study or competence who can then advise the rest of us.

more than the rest of their peers (and us), and their claims carry with them the weight of rational deliberation, insight, and brilliance.

What distinguishes geniuses from everyone else, Kierkegaard tells us, is the relative superiority of their natural endowments. Geniuses or experts are *more* brilliant, intelligent, and rational than we are, and this puts them in a better position to ascertain the truth. Geniuses, then, presumably have access to truths that the rest of us do not. They are ahead of the curve, so to speak, and have the capacity to leap ahead of the rest of us to make advances and new discoveries in human knowledge. Because of this, geniuses are also qualified to speak *authoritatively* about how the rest of us ought to believe, think, and act—even if we cannot quite understand them or personally access their evidence and arguments. But on closer look we see that the superiority of the genius is rather a tenuous arrangement, because there is also a kind of inevitability to a genius's discoveries. In theory, the rest of us *could* have made the discoveries, and if this particular genius had not made them, no doubt sooner or later another would have. In theory, the human race in general will catch up with the geniuses and surpass them by improving upon or adding to their insights, because what makes them geniuses are qualities they share with other humans. A genius, Kierkegaard notes, merely adds to the body of human knowledge and ingenuity, and eventually this is incorporated into the horizon of human potential.

What is interesting to me in Kierkegaard's analysis is the connection between the modern emphasis on genius and the modern concept of reason. Genius is the highest expression of human potential and reason, and it plays an authoritative role because of the secular condition of modernity. Once modernity frees itself from the premodern appeal to tradition and supernatural revelation, genius is really the only game left in town. Not only are the premodern sources of authority (tradition and revelation) seen to be unreliable by modern thinkers, but the entire picture of the world that makes them plausible and intelligible has been abandoned. At the end of the day, the modern appeal to genius (or expertise) as the final authority for belief and practice directly corresponds to the authority accorded human reason (as objective, universal, and neutral) to act as the ground or source of warrant for our beliefs. We trust geniuses and experts and treat them as authorities because they present us with the highest expression of what is reasonable for us to believe.

The apostle, however, appeals not to reason but to *revelation* as the basis on which claims are warranted. A genius is *born*, Kierkegaard points out, while an apostle is *called*. Whereas genius is a quality that distinguishes a person from other human beings comparatively—by being *more* rational or brilliant or intelligent—the apostle's constitutive identity comes from the *call of God*. Subsequently, the apostle's message is one that no one else can improve upon or add to because it is dependent on God's action alone. There is nothing extraordinary about apostles prior to their call to apostleship, and taken on their own, apostles are no greater than anyone else—and may even be inferior in certain ways. Apostleship does not depend on any particular human abilities. In this sense, every human being is equally capable of being an apostle, regardless of their circumstance or natural endowments—because the source is God.[4] At the same time, this is precisely what qualifies the claims of the apostle as authoritative and revelatory. The apostolic message does not have authority because it is demonstrably rational or exceptionally brilliant but because *it is a word from God*. God's word does not come to us as the result of human calculation or brilliance and cannot be improved upon, nor will it ever become obsolete.[5] The truths of revelation are not realities humans will inevitably discover through their research projects, nor will they be able to assimilate them into their collective potential. The claims of revelation are what Kierkegaard describes as a "paradox" to human reason, because they seemingly eclipse the rational reach

4. Kierkegaard follows St. Paul very closely in this discussion of apostleship, particularly Paul's letters to the Romans and the Corinthians (e.g., 1 Cor. 1:18–2:16). When Kierkegaard asserts that all humans are equally close to apostleship, he anticipates parts of Giorgio Agamben's discussion of Paul's apostolic *klēsis* (calling) and the egalitarian nature of the messianic call and vocation as a *hōs mē* (as not), in Giorgio Agamben, *The Time That Remains* (Stanford, CA: Stanford University Press, 2005), 22ff. "*Hōs mē*, 'as not': this is the formula concerning messianic life and is the ultimate meaning of *klēsis*. Vocation calls for nothing and to no place. For this reason it may coincide with the factical condition in which each person finds himself called" (23).

5. This does not commit Kierkegaard to a view of Christian revelation that rules out human involvement in the revelatory process. Rather, I am committing him to the view that insofar as something is revealed, it is in that respect from God.

of any human epistemic community—yet, as genuine truth claims, they are not utter nonsense to reason either.[6] This paradox, the difference or chasm that separates the human genius from divine truth, is generated by *sin*, which is irrational, alienating, and caused by the individual person.[7] However much human reason might be necessary to *understand* the apostolic proclamation (insofar as it qualifies as revelation), reason has no role to play whatsoever in *grounding* the apostle's claims. Therefore, the apostolic message cannot be made illegitimate or legitimate by demonstrations of its rational superiority.

An important part of Kierkegaard's distinction between a genius and an apostle is a critique of the modern conception of knowledge and its emphasis on science. To begin with, there is strong resonance between Kierkegaard's analysis and postmodern critiques of reason, particularly the "three masters of suspicion," as Paul Ricoeur calls them—Nietzsche, Marx, and Freud.[8] The view of reason that fits best with the apostle/genius distinction is one markedly different from the modern epistemological paradigm. On the one hand, the Christian concept of revelation—as a word from God—entails that any expression of human reason is less than adequate to ground the full truth, or the truth as it would appear to God.[9] The fact that revelation cannot be derived from any human capacities, especially human reason, means it is unable to ground the truths it discovers in any absolute or final way. The practice of justifying beliefs and actions using human

6. Kierkegaard, *Book on Adler*, 175–76. The claims of genius initially appear paradoxical in this sense, as they outstrip the current justificatory practices of their rational community. But ultimately, because they are based upon them (the language, concepts, and practices of the community), they are only paradoxical "in the inessential sense of the transitory paradox" (175) and eventually establish a new norm for the rational community.

7. Climacus in Søren Kierkegaard, *Philosophical Fragments*, ed. and trans. Howard V. Hong and Edna H. Hong (Princeton: Princeton University Press, 1985), 47.

8. Paul Ricoeur, *Freud and Philosophy: An Essay on Interpretation*, trans. Denis Savage (New Haven: Yale University Press, 1970), 33. The best introduction to the religious significance of Nietzsche, Freud, and Marx that I know of is Merold Westphal, *Suspicion and Faith: The Religious Uses of Modern Atheism* (New York: Fordham University Press, 1998).

9. I am not using truth in a technical way here. I am aware of the mistake of conflating the epistemic concepts of truth and justification and will deal more with the concept of truth later. In this discussion I refer to the concept of truth broadly as those propositions that we can *see* are true (or understand to be true or justify).

reason is a fallibilist exercise, which means any outcomes, solutions, or conclusions about their rational acceptability are always (in theory) provisional and potentially reversible.[10] Human reason simply gives us the best answer we have *so far*, and not anything like the final truth about the matter.

The genius/apostle distinction also suggests reason is historically situated (within time) and contextual; reason is not a timeless, universal, or unchanging judge that is unaffected by its concrete circumstances. Human reason is thoroughly immanent and as such does not occupy a transcendent perspective. It is not able to apprehend every moment, nor is it capable of grounding its truth claims absolutely. Kierkegaard is quite clear on this. A word from God may be transcendent, but human perspectives are not. Subsequently, Kierkegaard throws his support in for Hegel's view that the exercise of human reason is socially conditioned in the sense that our justifications need the mutual recognition of the communities in which we live in order for them to be perceived as authoritative (or count as rational). But Kierkegaard disagrees with Hegel that this, in the end, is able to produce a transcendent or absolute perspective for us.[11] There is no pure self-possession in which one's thoughts are transparent to oneself, and there is likewise no pure and absolute possession of truths, if by this we mean ideas or beliefs unconditioned and held from a perspectiveless vantage point. When we try to justify truths by appealing to a modern conception of human reason, we always do so from some contingent, particular point of view that is shaped in large part by some particular group's perspective. What counts for us as a justification is part and parcel of the social practices in which we engage. This is because the concepts and language we use to do so (and in which we think) are deeply embedded in our social practices.

10. Here we see Kierkegaard was himself a kind of genius, operating well ahead of the curve, for almost without exception contemporary epistemologists are fallibilists in this sense.

11. While this critique is certainly at work within the argument of *The Book on Adler*, it is even more clear in Søren Kierkegaard, *Two Ages: The Age of Revolution and the Present Age: A Literary Review*, ed. and trans. Howard V. Hong and Edna H. Hong (Princeton: Princeton University Press, 1978), especially 106–7. Cf. Kierkegaard's critique of Hegel's view of revelation as "the historicizing philosophy of identity," in Kierkegaard, *Book on Adler*, 119–21.

This discussion of genius, then, along with its view of human reason, connects to one of the constant refrains in Kierkegaard's texts, which concerns the way human reason is distorted by modern social groups whenever it is used to justify truth claims.[12] Genius, it will be remembered, is a distinction that is *relative*—specifically relative to the peers of the genius who are able to recognize the individual as a genius, and over against whom the individual is identified as genius. But we must also keep in mind that the insights of genius will soon be eclipsed by or assimilated into the collective knowledge and aspirations of the rest of us. Because the only legitimate appeal for justification in modernity is to human reason (viz., genius), and because human reason is situated in a particular context, the justification of beliefs deteriorates at some point into an appeal to "the crowd" or "the public" as the means of securing an agreement as to what really counts as rational.[13] Kierkegaard's discussion of genius, then, highlights for

12. See, for example, Søren Kierkegaard, *Concluding Unscientific Postscript to Philosophical Fragments*, 2 vols., ed. and trans. Howard V. Hong and Edna H. Hong (Princeton: Princeton University Press, 1992), 1.354–55, where Climacus rails against "the generation-idea" in modernity that justifies itself and its claims by appealing to "'we,' 'our age,' 'the nineteenth century,'" and which, in the name of truth and progress, completely undercuts the concerns and values—in short, the humanity—of human subjects. Merold Westphal, in *Kierkegaard's Critique of Reason and Society* (University Park, PA: Pennsylvania State University Press, 1991), 34, explains that "Kierkegaard seeks to unsocialize the individual in order to un-deify society." For more on this, see Merold Westphal, *Overcoming Onto-Theology* (New York: Fordham University Press, 2001), 154–55.

13. This point becomes more obvious when the genius/apostle distinction is read alongside Kierkegaard's critique of "the idea of sociality," modern "leveling," and "the public" in *Two Ages*, 106–7, but it must be drawn out carefully. Perhaps the best way to read Kierkegaard's genius/apostle distinction is through the lens of Hegel's "Lordship-Bondage" dialectic in *The Phenomenology of Spirit*, trans. J. B. Baillie (New York: Harper Torchbook, 1967), 228–40, which Hegel uses to establish the interdependence of self-consciousness on the other. In *The Book on Adler* the genius, as with Hegel's "master" or "lord," seemingly operates with indifference to the rest of humanity and sees her- or himself as superior to it. This is an affront to the rest of us ("bond-servants"), who both need the genius and want to be identified with him- or herself. However, the genius's self-satisfied superiority to peers and detachment from the rest of us is a self-deception. Ultimately, the genius has what Kierkegaard describes as an "immanent teleology" that is shared with the rest of humanity (the self-actualization of both self and the human race), and the genius and his or her accomplishments are doomed to disappear into the horizon of human "progress." Rather than being discontinuous with humanity, as the genius believes, the genius

us how the modern appeal to reason quickly moves from being the shared assumptions of some group to the self-legitimation of some established order that has a vested interest in the group's being right. Despite its prima facie originality and innovation, in the end genius collapses back on itself and has no authority, originality, or proficiency that does not come from the court of public opinion. There is no other way for genius to ground itself.

It is not difficult to discern behind the genius/apostle distinction the idea that, as Marx will later argue, in modernity reason quickly becomes *ideology*. Here I use "ideology" in reference to the nonrational (and oppressive) way the belief and value commitments of the dominant group of people in a society function to create a certain view of reality that is implicitly accepted as correct or true and explicitly enforced by instruments of social control.[14] The insidious and oppressive dimension of ideology is located in its tendency to treat individuals *en masse*, indifferent to their individual personhood (subjectivity). Genius cannot ground its claims in any way that is final or absolute outside of the rational consensus of "the power-craving crowd,"[15] which functions at the ideological level both to make truth claims legitimate *and* to produce them.

(unlike the apostle) is what he or she is precisely *because* of his continuity with the human race. There is, however, a constant and mutual antagonism between geniuses and the rest of us: geniuses want to transcend "the crowd" but ultimately cannot do without it, while the crowd needs the geniuses but always wants to subsume them by becoming like them. Subsequently, a culture of geniuses or experts lives in a perpetual legitimation crisis.

Kierkegaard posits that the apostle breaks this dialectic. Ironically, the very thing that separates an apostle from his or her peers (the call from God) is also what unites them: on the one hand, the apostolic message is something no human can own, improve upon, or sit in judgment over; yet, on the other hand, the transcendent nature of God's call places the apostle on the same level as the rest of his or her peers because the apostle does not ground or legitimate the message herself. See Kierkegaard, *Book on Adler*, 187–88.

14. Ideologies are identifiable primarily by their effect, which is to create a mass identity and provide a governing rationale for the practices of a society that translates into a program for action. Cf. Glenn Tinder, *The Political Meaning of Christianity: An Interpretation* (Baton Rouge, LA: Louisiana State University Press, 1989), 222. Whereas for Tinder ideologies are more explicit and consciously acknowledged doctrines designed to mobilize society as a whole for action, I see them as mostly implicit and functioning even when we are not aware of them.

15. Kierkegaard, *Book on Adler*, 188.

Put this way, the claims of genius are always destined to become some group's prevailing ideology, no matter how much they functioned at one point in time to challenge the group's consensus. If the modern claim is that reason functions as an authority for belief and practice, the Kierkegaardian genius/apostle distinction suggests that its ideological character fundamentally undercuts this claim. As it turns out, the products of human reason are as much the result of prejudice and bias as they are objective, universal, and neutral. What counts as rational is always embedded within a set of power relations operative within a given social structure. And rather than producing the untarnished truth about the way the world *really* is, human reason merely presents us with a series of perspectives that reflect the way the world appears to a group (or groups) of people. In this situation, it is hard for the claims of reason to avoid the slip into mass culture—with its mass production of cultural products, icons, and celebrities, and above all its dependence on mass media to shape perceptions, tastes, and values so that as many people in as many places as possible are perceiving reality in the same way. Legitimation for purchases, beliefs, values, perceptions are all justified in roughly the same way: by achieving the widest possible number of adherents. This allows us to assert that what we believe and do is obviously the most rational way of believing and acting.

Allow me to return to my earlier point of departure regarding Kierkegaard's critique of apologetics. One of the central insights of the genius/apostle distinction is that the modern world is inherently empty and meaningless—and thereby lacking in authority. The modern secular condition leaves us in a world yet to be rationalized and has no external reference points to ground it. Carl Raschke describes this in terms of "the monstrous secret of modernity" and links it to the concept of nihilism[16]—or the negative impulse that negates or denies the positive existence of concepts like truth, beauty, meaning, and even reality itself. Kierkegaard clearly perceives that the implications of modern secular reason are tantamount to the nihilism Nietzsche

16. Carl Raschke, *The Next Reformation: Why Evangelicals Must Embrace Postmodernity* (Grand Rapids: Baker Academic, 2004), 43.

later announces as the "death of God."[17] Rather than mounting an argument against believing in God's existence, Nietzsche's pronouncement of the death of God simply acknowledges that in the modern secular condition there is no longer any need to understand God apart from our own self-awareness.[18] When secular reason becomes the final ground of belief and practice, God only enters into our systems of belief on *our* terms—to justify them—and ultimately even our concept of God is merely symptomatic of our own conceptual systems. Raschke, then, is absolutely correct to emphasize that this incipient nihilism of modernity is *not* something that can be explained away as a kind of social malady produced by only a few fringe thinkers in modernity, who are philosophical radicals and intellectual extremists. Instead, nihilism is located right at the very heart of modernity as the result of its distinctive brand of secularity.[19] The privileging of geniuses means apostles lose their voice.

Viewed in light of the genius/apostle distinction, then, the problem with modern apologetics is that Christian thought has already given up

17. Nietzsche writes, "The greatest recent event—that 'God is dead'; that the belief in the Christian God has become unbelievable—is already starting to cast its first shadow over Europe." *The Gay Science*, ed. Bernard Williams, trans. Josefine Nauckhoff (Cambridge: Cambridge University Press, 2001), 200. Nietzsche published *The Gay Science* in 1882, while Kierkegaard first published "On the Difference between a Genius and an Apostle" some thirty-three years earlier. Raschke, *Next Reformation*, 42, locates the origin of the concept of the "death of God" back in Hegel's *Phenomenology* (published in 1807). No doubt Raschke is thinking of a passage toward the end of the *Phenomenology*, where Hegel states: "The Divine Being is reconciled with its existence through an event—the event of God's emptying Himself of His Divine Being through His factual Incarnation and His Death . . . what dies is not the outer encasement, which, being stripped of essential Being, is also, *eo ipso* dead, but also the abstraction of the Divine Being. . . . The death of this pictorial idea implies at the same time the death of the abstraction of Divine Being, which is not yet affirmed as a self. That death is the bitterness of feeling of the 'unhappy consciousness,' when it feels that God Himself is dead" (780–82).

18. Raschke, *Next Reformation*, 42.

19. If this is true, Douglas Groothuis, *Truth Decay: Defending Christianity Against the Challenges of Postmodernity* (Downers Grove, IL: InterVarsity, 2002), 42, completely misdiagnoses the source and nature of contemporary nihilism when he argues that it is postmodernism, not modernism, that is nihilistic. Of course, some postmodern thinkers are nihilistic, but only when they accept the inevitability of the modern secular condition and treat the incipient nihilism of modernity as a fait accompli. For postmodernists, our nihilism tends to be a descriptive reality of the inner logic of modernity, not a prescriptive position for which we are trying to argue.

far too much by merely acknowledging and responding to the modern challenges to Christian belief, as if these objections had some sort of claim on the legitimacy of faith. Kierkegaard is not against apologetics because he is a fideist who thinks Christian belief negates human reason, or that faith is opposed to any critical reflection on beliefs whatsoever. He objects to the entire modern epistemological paradigm that produces modern apologetics, because it attempts to ground faith in genius or secular reason. Modernity thereby empties faith of its Christian content and robs it of its authority.[20] In this way the genius/apostle distinction suggests modern apologetics is *itself* a symptom of the incipient nihilism at the core of modern thought, insofar as it implicitly accepts and emerges from the modern paradigm. Thus, the problem with modern apologetics is it does nothing to challenge or help us cope with modern nihilism. That is the significance of Kierkegaard's repeated attacks on modern apologetics, and this insight is at the very core of what it means to be against apologetics.

Apologetic Nihilism

Contemporary debates over the reasonableness of Christianity only reinforce this sense of the implicit nihilism of modern apologetics. The most recent adversaries for Christian apologists today are the "New Atheists," as *Wired* magazine has called them. These New Atheists are a group of scientific and philosophical experts who have launched a publishing *blitzkrieg* in an all-out "war against faith."[21] The apologetic establishment has launched a retaliatory strike, rallying its own army of experts to publish myriad articles and books in a theistic counterattack.[22] The two sides even collaborate to take

20. Cf. Raschke, *Next Reformation*, 44.
21. Gary Wolf, "The Church of the Non-Believers," *Wired*, November 2006, http://www.wired.com/wired/archive/14.11/atheism_pr.html. Some of the more popular publications of the New Atheists are Sam Harris, *The End of Faith: Religion, Terror, and the Future of Reason* (New York: W. W. Norton, 2005); Christopher Hitchens, *God Is Not Great: How Religion Poisons Everything* (New York: Twelve, 2007); Daniel C. Dennett, *Breaking the Spell: Religion as a Natural Phenomenon* (New York: Penguin, 2007); and Richard Dawkins, *The God Delusion* (Boston: Mariner Books, 2008).
22. For just a smattering, see William Lane Craig and Chad Meister, eds., *God Is Good, God Is Great: Why Believing in God Is Reasonable and Responsible* (Downers

the show on the road with publicized debate tours,[23] during which
the New Atheists and Christian apologists rehearse their positions
and arguments in front of large crowds—often televised with high
production values. In these situations it is very difficult for me to
avoid the assumption—conditioned, I suppose, by experiences like
the one described at the outset of this chapter—that these crowds
already have their minds made up before the debates occur and that
the events themselves do little to change anyone's mind.

But the utterly astonishing feature of these apologetic exhibitions
is the level of agreement between the atheists and the theists, at both
the philosophical and the ideological levels. British literary theorist
Terry Eagleton points out that in many ways the Christian apologists
and the New Atheists are, in fact, mirror images of each other.[24] Faith
for either side boils down to a kind of positive scientific knowledge
that tends to reduce the substance of faith to an intellectual debate
over the reasonableness of a theoretical entity: the proposition "God
exists."[25] Eagleton argues, for example, that when the New Atheists
point out there are several things in the Bible that may not or could

Grove, IL: InterVarsity, 2009); John F. Haught, *God and the New Atheism: A Critical
Response to Dawkins, Harris, and Hitchens* (Louisville: Westminster John Knox Press,
2008); Scott Hahn and Benjamin Wiker, *Answering the New Atheism: Dismantling
Dawkins's Case Against God* (Steubenville, OH: Emmaus Road Publishing, 2008);
Phillip E. Johnson and John Mark Reynolds, *Against All Gods: What's Right and
Wrong about the New Atheism* (Downers Grove, IL: InterVarsity, 2010); and R. Al-
bert Mohler Jr., *Atheism Remix: A Christian Confronts the New Atheists* (Wheaton:
Crossway, 2008).
    23. William Lane Craig's debates with the "New Atheists" are easily accessible
online.
    24. Terry Eagleton, *Reason, Faith, and Revolution: Reflections on the God Debate*
(New Haven: Yale University Press, 2009), 53. For virtually the same claim, see Slavoj
Žižek, *In Defense of Lost Causes* (New York: Verso, 2008), 114.
    25. It is true that no Christian apologist I know of believes that the proposition
"God exists"—or any other proposition for that matter—encapsulates a fully orbed
life of faith and everything it means to be a Christian. Nevertheless, it is also true
that the full life of faith is understood by these apologists to be grounded on that very
proposition (as the rational warrant for the full life of faith). Thus, to that degree,
the life of faith is reducible to this proposition. It is the narrow way through which
any legitimate faith must pass and is so closely tied to the life of faith that it becomes
difficult on the apologists' construal to imagine genuine faith in any other terms. And
if actual practice indicates anything, "God exists" certainly is the central focus of the
vast majority of the apologetic debates and arguments.

not have happened, as if this is a serious problem for Christian faith, it "is rather like someone vehemently trying to convince you, with fastidious attention to architectural and zoological detail, that King Kong could not possibly have scaled the Empire State Building because it would have collapsed under his weight."[26] And instead of pointing out that the relations between the current state of scientific theory and historical fact in Scripture is exceedingly complex, and an emphasis on the rational standards of secular modernity points us in the wrong direction, the apologetic response is to argue feverishly that the architectural and engineering practices of the early twentieth century have been completely misunderstood by the New Atheists, and that the mass of a body with King Kong's physical proportions could, in fact, be supported by the Empire State Building—with the assumption nothing else is needed to see this other than the pure light of human reason.

I find it equally striking that both the Christian apologists and the New Atheists see themselves as locked in a high-stakes culture war for the hearts and minds of society. New Atheist Richard Dawkins is keenly aware of "the politics of persuading people of the virtues of atheism," and likens being an atheist today to being gay a few decades ago: "There was a need for people to come out. The more people who came out, the more people had the courage to come out."[27] He therefore sees his vocation as making it easy for atheists to "come out," hoping to change the recent tide of Western culture and make it rationally possible for people to openly confess their atheism. And William Lane Craig readily admits to the ideological dimension of Christian apologetics. Just when one might expect Craig to appeal to encountering truth or maybe even rationality, he describes his apologetic debates at universities in terms of "a Westernized version of what missiologists call a '*power encounter*,'" because of their capacity to shape the minds and attitudes of young people and counteract the power the prevailing ideologies of our culture have

26. Eagleton, *Reason, Faith, and Revolution*, 54.
27. Richard Dawkins in an interview with Gary Wolf, "The Church of the Non-Believers," *Wired*, November 2006, http://www.wired.com/wired/archive/14.11/atheism_pr.html.

over them.[28] As a matter of fact, Craig's express intention is to shape culture through these apologetic debates. His hope is apologetics will establish a dominant "Christian" culture that acknowledges *his* particular propositional construal of Christian faith as *the* correct one. And anything that jeopardizes that hegemony is marginalized and denounced as a satanic plot![29]

But are not these culture-shaping intentions of the current God Debate, then, a prime illustration of how the appeal to genius (experts) turns into ideology? And when these apologetic debates and dissertations on the relative merits of dis/believing in God turn to mass media and culture-production as the means of spreading their message or bolstering their cause, do they not undermine the avowed objective, rational character of the entire debate? In the end, these exercises of "reason" seem to function in a manner that is virtually indistinguishable from ideological power plays. We—the "power-crazed crowd," as Kierkegaard would say—become a law and reason unto ourselves: *we* determine what is reasonable, *we* decide the correct form of belief, and *we* assume the right to label those who disagree with us not only as ignorant and irrational but also as immoral and depraved.[30]

The paradoxical result of the modern apologetic defense of Christianity, then, is that when God's existence is established according to

28. William Lane Craig, *Reasonable Faith: Christian Faith and Apologetics*, 3rd ed. (Wheaton: Crossway, 2008), 21 (my emphasis). Craig believes a key function of Christian apologetics is to "train our kids for war" before we send them out into our culture—e.g., "public high school" and "university" (19). He says "we are in danger of losing our youth" and we need to learn to keep them in the faith by teaching them doctrine and apologetics (19). "Frankly," Craig states, "I find it difficult to understand how people today can risk parenthood without having studied apologetics" (19).

29. Craig, *Reasonable Faith*, 18. As we noted in chap. 1, Craig says this in reference to postmodern proposals—like mine—that deemphasize the nature and role of a modern conception of reason in defending the faith.

30. We saw this disposition displayed in chap. 1, in the invective of J. P. Moreland, who uses these exact words to describe *Christians* who do not adhere to his version of modern apologetic Christianity. "Truth, Contemporary Philosophy and the Postmodern Turn," *Journal of the Evangelical Theological Society* 48 (2005): 77–88. The ideological dimensions of Moreland's overt attempt to "gate-keep" for his academic community are glaringly obvious. So much so that Moreland's performance undercuts his central claim that truth is ontological (not epistemic) and should be understood in terms of a correspondence theory. His piece is almost transparently ideological. See Myron B. Penner, "Cartesian Anxiety, Perspectivalism, and Truth: A Response to J. P. Moreland," *Philosophia Christi* 8, no. 1 (2006): 85–98, for my full response to Moreland.

modern secular reason, all that really is demonstrated is the dispens-
ability of anything that resembles belief in God. Believing in God is
less about the worship of God disclosed to us through a tradition and
a historic community called the church, and more about how theistic
belief is rationally predictable within the limits of modern secular
reason.[31] In this case, it becomes possible to rationalize anything,
perhaps (*except* God!). Furthermore, our most important and basic
values—including truth itself and human reason—are themselves
"trans-valued" and devaluate themselves.[32] Modern thought effectively kills God and, ironically, reason dies along with God. Speaking
theologically, we could say that accepting the modern paradigm as
I have described it is tantamount to conceptual idolatry and methodological blasphemy. And far from counteracting modern nihilism,
the apologetic responses to the New Atheists often seem to only add
more twists to the Nietzschean declaration of God's death. God is not
permitted to speak on God's own terms, so belief must be coaxed and
cajoled from the crowd in terms they find acceptable and appealing.

Not to be overlooked in this discussion of modern apologetic nihilism are the implications of the God Debate as a well-paying *industry*,
with books, videos, seminars—even academic positions, programs,
and institutions[33]—as blue-chip commodities. Jean Baudrillard focuses a great deal of attention on the material aspects of the modern
secular condition and attempts to show how the social, cultural, and
economic practices of modernity display its theoretical nihilism in
concrete, material terms.[34] Products and commodities take the place

31. Creston Davis nicely describes the logic of this position in his "Introduction:
Holy Saturday or Resurrection? Staging an Unholy Debate," in John Milbank and
Slavoj Žižek, *The Monstrosity of Christ*, ed. Creston Davis (Cambridge, MA: MIT
Press, 2009), 8–11.
32. Compare Carl Raschke's florid account of Nietzsche's concept of nihilism and
its relation to contemporary Christian thought in Raschke, *Next Reformation*, 43–45.
33. Try being a Christian creationist professor at Oxford University or Harvard
University, or an atheist evolutionist professor at Biola University or Liberty University.
34. Incidentally, for Baudrillard postmodernity is the situation in which the nihilism
(or meaninglessness) of modernity is consciously appropriated and lived out. See Jean
Baudrillard, *Simulacra and Simulation*, trans. Sheila Faria Glaser (Ann Arbor, MI:
University of Michigan Press, 1994), 159–61. So Douglas Groothuis, *Truth Decay*,
41–42, is both correct to describe postmodernity in terms of this nihilism and incorrect at the same time. He is right to link postmodernity to modernity in Baudrillard's

of God in modern life by becoming the focus of our lives and giving them "meaning." And as these products are increasingly commodified, mass-produced, and redistributed, the disappearance and "evanescence" of products—their absence—becomes an important part of maintaining the status quo. In other words, commodities are meant to be consumed and are disappearing constantly. We do not mass-produce products in order to create permanent artifacts. Ours is a world of simulacra and hyperreality, and we live with a continuous barrage of images that appear and then disappear. As this occurs, Baudrillard observes, meaning (and God) are also increasingly absent from our lives. We might call this a performative nihilism that performs or *displays* our secular condition and leaves us with a deep sense of the absence of God, meaning, or any substantial reality.

The effects of this performative nihilism on our systems of justification and legitimation are described by Baudrillard in *The System of Objects* as being driven by "the logic of Father Christmas."[35] Most of us are not fully conscious of this peculiar logic, which makes our media so effective in selling products and beliefs to us. It is not a logic of propositions and proofs per se, but "a logic of fables and of the willingness to go along with them."[36] One of the basic truths Baudrillard identifies about the way we justify our production of commodities and our buying of them—usually to great excess—is that now these objects are not meant so much to be owned and used as they are to be produced and bought.[37] So we tend to hold our beliefs about

thought, but he is wrong to think that for Baudrillard the nihilism of postmodernity radicalizes or demonizes something essentially good in modernity. Where Groothuis runs into problems in his use of Baudrillard to define postmodernity is that he persistently views Baudrillard as *arguing* for postmodernity *prescriptively*—which, of course, means that the nihilism Baudrillard describes can (and perhaps should) be argued with and refuted. However, Baudrillard—like Nietzsche—repeatedly claims merely to be *describing* his situation, his context. See, for example, Baudrillard, *Simulacra and Simulation*, 160–61: "I am a nihilist. I observe, I accept, I assume the immense process of the destruction of appearances . . . in the service of meaning . . . that is the fundamental fact of the nineteenth century. . . . I observe, I accept, I assume, I analyze the second revolution, that of the twentieth century, that of postmodernity, which is the immense process of the destruction of meaning, equal to the earlier destruction of appearances."

35. Jean Baudrillard, *The System of Objects* (New York: Verso, 1996), 180–81.

36. Ibid., 180.

37. Ibid., 176.

our products like children who hardly ever wonder whether Father Christmas exists, and certainly never consider getting presents as an effect of the actual existence of Santa Claus. Advertising for a product—and one might extend this to other facets of demonstration in our media[38]—does not really convince us of the product's worth and often does not even pretend to try to do that. These "demonstrations" serve merely to rationalize our purchases. "Without 'believing' in the product, therefore, we believe in the advertising that tries to get us to believe in it."[39]

This type of situation, Baudrillard explains, generates "the surplus of meaning."[40] The primary competition between rival claims in this arena is not really over the truth or the range of explanatory power—that is, at the level of "meaning" or "truth"—but at the socioeconomic level over the range of acceptance. The goal is to win as many adherents as possible. Meaning and truth are secondary to the discourse—a kind of surplus that is increasingly irrelevant. What really keeps the discourse and debate going is the act of the debate itself, almost without our remembering why the debate is happening in the first place. This phenomenon precedes and aids the creation of temporary, disappearing commodities and the spread of indifference. "The desert grows."[41]

The contemporary God Debate seems to generate its own surplus of meaning, with its debate tours, media products, blog sites, and YouTube videos. Dis/believing in God has gone viral, and the primary point might appear to be the effective marketing of the product—to get people to believe in the advertising, to win adherents. In this situation, is it possible that the God Debates contribute to the "implosion of meaning" Baudrillard describes, and threaten to render the entire issue of God's existence essentially mute and meaningless—a little like our "belief" in Father Christmas? And when Christians engage in these debates or "defenses" of the faith, do they not risk relegating

38. For example, this mechanism is what drives Jon Stewart's and Stephen Colbert's parody of the news. Stewart and Colbert reveal that our production of news is a commodity whose primary goal is not to inform us but entertain us. In this sense, they might be the most honest source of news.
39. Baudrillard, *System of Objects*, 180–81.
40. Baudrillard, *Simulacra and Simulation*, 161.
41. Ibid.

Christian belief to the level of a consumer product that is bought and sold? Gaining the widest possible adherence certainly appears to be the express purpose of apologetics. And there seems to be an almost pathological drive for apologetic experts to publish another book or article containing "new" arguments, new refutations, and new responses. Consumer demand is high for more apologetics experts to write more books, conduct more seminars, and teach more courses. So we also have to train more apologetics experts who are qualified to disseminate the objectively true propositions, arguments, and evidence so that we may demonstrate the truth about Christian faith by creating a wider culture of belief than of disbelief. Thus there is a drive to commodify and mass-produce apologetic products so they can be distributed, consumed, and reproduced again, which ultimately is the means of producing an objective Christian culture of belief. Of course, this requires an objective culture of disbelief as a necessary backdrop.

The situation is not unlike the one portrayed in G. K. Chesterton's *The Man Who Was Thursday*. Here the head of the anti-anarchist police corps, whose sole objective is to infiltrate and dismantle the European anarchist council, is discovered, in the end, to be the same supercriminal who has developed and runs the European anarchist council. The highest police authority is really just staging a battle with himself.[42] Similarly, it appears that what is being resisted or fought as the external threat in the God Debate is the mirror image of itself and that the danger to faith emanates from its own inherent essence (and vice versa). To be sure, there is subterfuge, agents are deployed, battles are fought with real casualties, but it is not clear where the *real* threat is coming from. The apologetics industry can only exist in conditions of permanent threat and therefore has a vested interest in maintaining a permanent state of emergency.

At the social and economic level, then, the contemporary God Debate at the very least raises the question of whether it really matters why or how one believes or disbelieves at all. Given the way in which these debates are conducted and commodified, and given the

42. Cf. Slavoj Žižek, who connects *The Man Who Was Thursday* to the M. Night Shyamalan movie *The Village*, but puts them to work for a different purpose than mine. *Violence: Six Sideways Reflections* (New York: Picador, 2008), 27.

way they play off each other, the wider message might appear to be: "The reasons you believe are really not important; what is important is that you *spend*.[43] Buy the books, the podcasts, and the tickets for the debates, lectures, and seminars; pay for your kids' tuition at certain schools and universities. *An entire way of life* (i.e., mode of consumption) *and industry is at stake*, not to mention academic careers and tenure (for the experts on both sides)!" This is exactly the kind of process Baudrillard—being the nihilist he is—celebrates as "our own mode of destroying finalities."[44] When this happens, "defending the faith" borders on a nihilistic performance that at minimum should elicit some care and concern among Christians over the cultural and social implications of these dimensions of the apologetic industry.

Fallibilism and Hermeneutics

It should be clear now why I stated in the introduction to this book that if we are to take the Kierkegaardian critique of apologetics seriously in a postmodern context, we will need *an entirely new way of conceiving the apologetic task*. One of the serious problems for modern apologetics is that it treats Christianity as if it were an objective "something" (e.g., a set of propositions or doctrines) that can be explained, proven, and cognitively mastered.[45] Kierkegaard's favorite response is to point out that being a Christian is far less a matter of *knowing* the truth than that of *becoming* the truth—that is, of *being truly* rather than *thinking truly*—so that the truth is expressed in a fully integrated life before God. Christianity, then, is much more a *way* or an invitation to live (walk, grow) in the truth than it is a doctrine or set of beliefs (a position) whose truth we can grasp and cognitively master, as the modern apologetic paradigm seems to imply.

43. There are echoes here of George Bush's urging of Americans to respond to the September 11, 2001, attacks by continuing to spend money and go shopping.
44. Baudrillard, *Simulacra and Simulation*, 161.
45. However, it is important also to note that Kierkegaard believes Christianity *has* doctrines, beliefs, etc., that are essential to its expression. See Myron B. Penner, "The Normative Resources of Kierkegaard's Subjectivity Principle," *International Journal of Systematic Theology* 1 (March 1999): 73–88.

The Kierkegaardian distinction between a genius and an apostle not only provides a substantial critique of the modern apologetic paradigm and its culture of experts, but also suggests an alternative to it. The critical moment in the genius/apostle distinction is its insistence on the utterly transcendent source of the apostle's call. This places us in what might be called an irremediable hermeneutical situation. Human reason cannot epistemically master the apostolic message, nor can it improve upon it or assimilate it into a wider theory of anything. The revelation is proclaimed and it is ours to *understand* and *interpret*, but not to justify or rationalize directly in the sense of establishing its legitimacy. Of course, questions about legitimacy may arise as one wrestles with cognitive and existential difficulties encountered in life, but they are questions that occur *within* the context of the received revelation, not wider questions of justification. To ask fundamental questions about legitimacy in the sense demanded by the modern epistemic paradigm requires wholesale conversion to some other interpretive framework, according to which the revelation in question is improbable.

Even the ability to recognize someone as an apostle depends upon an interpretive tradition—with a set of beliefs and practices, categories, values, goals, etc.—that makes sense of apostles and conceptually allows for them. In this way, it becomes possible to discern an implicit argument in the genius/apostle distinction for a view of human reason as fallible, finite, and situated. We will need to acknowledge that human beings are not adequate, in and of ourselves, to discover the most important truths about ourselves, others, God, or the world we inhabit. Our rational capacities have an open wound that must constantly be acknowledged and must continually give way to a word from God. In order to accommodate this, we will need to shift from an epistemological approach to something like a hermeneutical one.

Stanley Cavell addresses at least part of the hermeneutical move I have in mind when he writes that he "wished to understand philosophy not as a set of problems, but as a set of texts."[46] What Cavell means here is not the rather naive (and prosaic) assertion that philosophy

46. Stanley Cavell, *The Claim of Reason: Wittgenstein, Skepticism, Morality, and Tragedy* (Oxford: Oxford University Press, 1982), 3.

should be read as (mere) literature and that he attempts to understand philosophy as if it were not about problems at all. Instead, Cavell is saying the problems of philosophy are contextual in the strict sense of arising out of and being embodied in a set of texts as part of a historical tradition—as a type of cultural conversation that is carried on by a living community through its texts and practices. Cavell calls us to understand these problems textually and contextually in a way that entails they be treated in a different mode than typical modern philosophical analysis.[47] In other words, Cavell's approach to philosophy as a set of texts challenges the epistemological paradigm of modernity and effects a shift to a *hermeneutical* paradigm.

I want to think of theology and Christian belief hermeneutically, as Cavell views philosophy: as a set of texts that are part of the ongoing conversation of a widening community of people (i.e., the church). If the modern epistemological paradigm is focused on the question, "Is it (belief about the world/reality) true and justified?" the hermeneutical paradigm I want to replace it with puts at the center of its inquiry the question, "Is it *intelligible* and *meaningful*?" The pressing issue is not solving an abstract set of theoretical problems but interpreting the symbols and texts of a received tradition in order to understand their meaning and significance in relation to a concrete set of problems and exigencies that we encounter. A hermeneutical approach is better construed in terms of the metaphors of conversation and dialogue, as opposed to the epistemological model of trial and debate.[48] By definition, dialogue is bidirectional and other-centered; dominance and control are not compatible with it.[49] To be sure, there will be arguments, logic, evidence, and so on that are crucial parts of the process of arriving at conclusions within interpretive traditions, but these are invitations for response from differing points of view rather than an attempt to foreclose on them. These alternate points of view

47. Cf. Simon Critchley, *Continental Philosophy: A Very Short Introduction* (Oxford: Oxford University Press, 2001), 56.
48. David K. Clark also makes this observation in regard to apologetics. However, Clark continues to think of dialogue as a feature of epistemological discourse, emphasizing the need "to explore the ground, structure, and rationale" of the competing worldviews of the dialogue partners. *Dialogical Apologetics: A Person-Centered Approach* (Grand Rapids: Baker Books, 1993), 117.
49. Cf. Clark, *Dialogical Apologetics*, 116.

that emerge through dialogue are not barriers to understanding but enable us to gain greater insight into the text (as well as ourselves, our world, and others) as we submit our interpretations to critical tests that are free and open to critique and response.[50]

Perhaps even more important, critical reflection in a hermeneutical paradigm is focused on and grounded in our everyday practices and claims. It subjects our practices and claims to rigorous examination for their explanatory power and fidelity.[51] Epistemological issues do not drop out of view altogether, and, in fact, hermeneutics in the sense I mean can be construed as a *type* of epistemology.[52] It remains concerned with beliefs, truth, meaning, and a host of other epistemological questions, because most of its basic concepts contribute to intelligibility and meaning.

But there is another deeper and more basic hermeneutical element at work in my Kierkegaardian critique of apologetics that connects to Paul Ricoeur's insight that hermeneutic inquiry essentially involves the "art of deciphering *indirect* meaning."[53] As Kierkegaard notes, the incarnation in which God becomes a human—Jesus of Nazareth—is the founding event of Christianity and the central proclamation of its revelation. God—the transcendent, eternal, omnipotent creator of the universe—appears inside the creation as part of it. The truly remarkable and supernatural aspect of this is that God can undergo this incognito—as this particular man, Jesus—and be unrecognizable to the natural eye.[54] This, as I see it, is what provides Christians a central insight into the basic structure of human reason and its relation to the world. In a world of incarnation, truth can only appear to reason as paradox—that is to say, *indirectly*.

50. Cf. Kevin J. Vanhoozer, *First Theology: God, Scripture and Hermeneutics* (Downers Grove, IL: InterVarsity, 2002), 348n30.

51. See Paul Ricoeur, *Time and Narrative*, vol. 1, trans. Kathleen McLaughlin and David Pellauer (Chicago: University of Chicago Press, 1984), especially 91.

52. See Merold Westphal, "Hermeneutics as Epistemology," in *The Blackwell Guide to Epistemology*, ed. John Greco and Ernest Sosa (Oxford: Blackwell, 1999), 416–20, and Vanhoozer, *First Theology*, 345–48.

53. Cited in Richard Kearney, *On Paul Ricoeur: The Owl of Minerva* (Burlington, VT: Ashgate, 2004), 1.

54. The divine incognito is central to Anti-Climacus's argument in Kierkegaard, *Practice in Christianity*, ed. and trans. Howard V. Hong and Edna H. Hong (Princeton: Princeton University Press, 1991), especially 127–33; Climacus also discusses this in Kierkegaard, *Philosophical Fragments*, 23–36.

Since the incarnation of God involves a juxtaposition of such paradoxical elements as eternity in time and the infinite in the finite, it is not a truth that can appear to us directly. The upshot of the incarnation is that we now see God as fully here in ordinary life in a way that runs contrary to our "natural" expectations or what our rational deliberations demand. And yet, God also appears in our world in such a way that he cannot be identified completely with the medium (and manner) in which he appears. What must not be overlooked is that there is no other way for God to appear within the horizon of our situation as human beings.[55] Conceptually, interpretation is demanded by the Christian message from the very outset. This is an essential attribute of the apostle as one who is called by God to proclaim a revelation from God.

What marks off the hermeneutical paradigm from the modern epistemological one is its emphasis on the embodied, contextual nature of human reasoning and understanding. In one sense, of course, hermeneutics is a kind of epistemology—at least insofar as it is a reflection on the nature and limits of human knowledge.[56] However, as Ricoeur notes, the "first problem" for hermeneutics "is not how to get started, but from the midst of speech to recollect itself."[57] The focus is on texts, as the representation or codifying of speech-acts in written symbols (language), and understanding their meaning and interpretations and how they speak to our problems and issues today. Hermeneutics in this sense does not focus on abstract philosophical problems or on establishing an epistemological ground zero from which to launch an absolutely certain body of knowledge or to guarantee the rationality of belief. In other words, hermeneutics begins from *within* language and representation—with what has already been said and understood—and not from the pure, presuppositionless starting point that may act as the theoretical ground for knowledge.

55. This is one of the central arguments of Kierkegaard's *Philosophical Fragments*, but see especially 23–36. As John Milbank notes, Kierkegaard is making the Augustinian point that "a miracle is only a sign that has to be interpreted." "The Double Glory, or Paradox Versus Dialectics: On Not Quite Agreeing with Slavoj Žižek," in Milbank and Žižek, *The Monstrosity of Christ*, 211.

56. Westphal, "Hermeneutics as Epistemology," 416.

57. Paul Ricoeur, "The Hermeneutics of Symbols and Philosophical Reflection," in *The Philosophy of Paul Ricoeur: An Anthology of His Work*, ed. Charles E. Reagan and David Stewart (Boston: Beacon, 1978), 36.

Understood hermeneutically, then, human reason always operates within a specific theoretical, physical, and social environment, including a constitutive set of practices. Reason is useful to us when employed to understand where and how we live, but is "suspended" (or limited) in this paradigm, as it does not plumb the depths of reality, nor is it capable of functioning as a context-free judge or standard for human belief and action. The human capacity to reason is a helpful—and indispensable—tool that helps us navigate our lives, but its value is firmly rooted in the social practices that give it its theater of operations and in the language through which we express ourselves in them.

It is important to note, perhaps, that the Judeo-Christian tradition has *always* and *essentially* been hermeneutical in both its literary and philosophical senses. First, the Hebrew-Christian tradition has always been *textual* in the rather straightforward literary sense that it is focused on interpreting a received set of texts (God's Word) within a community that receives them. Interpretation of the Word of or from God is the fundamental intellectual activity of the Hebrew and Christian traditions. Hebrew-Christian reflection always begins with a received body of texts and speech-acts through which God has spoken. This basic Christian hermeneutical practice of interpreting Hebrew-Christian texts can also be understood as the practice Alasdair MacIntyre has in mind when he describes a conception of rational inquiry that is embodied in a tradition and in which the standards of rational justification emerge from the history and practice of interpretation within the rational community itself.[58]

Second, the Judeo-Christian tradition is also hermeneutical in the philosophical sense. It has its origins in *revelation*—with an event expressed in language (text) that is interpreted within the tradition and not by means of rational "first principles" (Greek philosophy). Ours is the God-who-*speaks* and *reveals*. The first moment of critical reflection in this tradition, then, is to wait and listen—to *hear* from God. Subsequently, the Judeo-Christian *logos* (word, reason) is one that always

58. Alasdair MacIntyre, *Whose Justice? Which Rationality?* (Notre Dame, IN: University of Notre Dame Press, 1988), 7. I am not saying that this has always been Christian self-understanding. As we shall see later, I do not mean this to indicate a universal form of rationality (as MacIntyre means), but that the Christian tradition creates the conditions for its intelligibility and interpretation.

exhausts human reason and always comes to us from the outside. It is never a word (a reason) that rests on human rational capacities, but displays the circular relation between believing and understanding that Ricoeur identifies as the basic character of hermeneutics.[59] Historically, Christian faith has always embodied (or at very least sits quite comfortably with) the truth that "we can believe only by interpreting."[60]

Hermeneutics may, of course, be yet another form of idolatry if all it does is provide a rule to establish what one *cannot* believe, and thereby transforms into yet another celebration of human reason—only in terms of its limitations. The temptation is merely to perpetuate the sins of modernity by continuing to worship method, only in the obverse: now that we are "enlightened" as to the errors of the Enlightenment, we have found *the* method of avoiding method, belief, truth, or commitment. While the hermeneutic approach to Christian faith has no exclusive purchase on truth and cannot guarantee that one will avoid cognitive idolatry, it at least has the benefit of acknowledging our (post)modern situation and providing us with a means of coping with the intellectual and spiritual malaise of the modern epistemological paradigm. The *life of faith*, however, is the primary thing.

Conclusion

So far I have made the unsettling suggestion that Christians should be against apologetics, at least of the modern variety. I am against the apologetic culture of experts that is funded by the modern secular condition, with its assumption that genius is the highest authority for belief and the reasonability of a belief—and my ability to demonstrate it—is the only thing that makes something worthy of my acceptance. I am also against the notion that our task as Christians is to demonstrate the intellectual superiority of Christian belief—as if we are Christians by dint of our genius. And finally, I am against the apologetic mind-set that sets "us" against "them" and then proceeds to try to win the marketing and merchandising race so that "our" superiority is thereby unquestioned.

59. Paul Ricoeur, *The Symbolism of Evil*, trans. Emerson Buchanan (Boston: Beacon, 1967), 352.
60. Ibid.

My strategy to this point has been "deconstructive" in that I have tried to show how modern epistemology and its assumptions about human reason are merely one culture's story about reason and belief, which ultimately devolves into ideology.[61] Left to itself, the modern epistemological paradigm collapses in on itself and does not present us with anything like the final, authoritative word on reason, belief, or knowledge—let alone faith. I have also tried to show that modern apologetics is parasitically attached to and symptomatic of the epistemological paradigm of modernity and doubly "deconstructs" itself. Not only does modern apologetics suffer the same troubles as modern philosophy, but the problem is compounded when it idolatrously perpetuates the "death of God" by treating human reason as the source and ground of its discourse.

To sum up, I am against apologetics because its modern forms undercut the very gospel it wishes to protect. The lesson I take from Kierkegaard's careful account of the difference between a genius and an apostle is that when the modern epistemological paradigm treats human reason as the source and ground for truth—as a replacement for a premodern reliance on God and other sources of belief outside oneself—then our most important values, such as God, truth, meaning, and even reason itself, are undermined. Genius cannot authorize much of anything, at the end of the day. Christianity has nothing to fear from genius and the "tough questions" of faith, simply because faith is not a matter of settling all the issues first, or rationally justifying all our beliefs before we accept them. That scenario belies a certain modern fixation on rational mastery that is a chimera. Subsequently, modern apologetics becomes a symptom of the modern epistemological paradigm. And not only does modern apologetics have no substantial way of addressing the modern secular condition that erodes belief in God, it may actually perpetuate forms of modern nihilism by accepting the basic assumptions that drive it. Philosophically this is problematic, theologically it flirts with conceptual idolatry, while practically it is unhelpful—it is what Kierkegaard and Rorty call "unedifying."

We are in some respects, then, caught between the rock of modernity and the hard place of the premodern worldview. Premodernity,

---

61. Westphal, *Overcoming Onto-Theology*, 133, 154.

with its hierarchical universe and naive picture of the world, is simply no longer viable, but we are also far too aware of the problems of the modern paradigm to find its program tenable. A shift to a hermeneutical approach to Christian faith, like the kind I propose, carefully negotiates faith in reference to the texts and traditions out of which we hear the apostles and prophets speak. It acknowledges that hearing God speak is an event that occurs in the context of a faithful community and requires careful and rigorous interpretation. It also accepts the fact that sometimes we get it wrong and there are often multiple layers of meaning at work, which produce a conflict of interpretations. These differing viewpoints must be worked out with fear and trembling, as there is no absolute zero-point from which we may judge once and for all the rightness or wrongness of our perspectives. Adopting a hermeneutical paradigm, however, does not leave us shiftless and rootless. In fact, there is a sense in which a hermeneutical approach leaves us much *more* rooted—in a community, in oneself, in God—but without the (illusory) modern appeal to an objective ground that is rationally coercive. Human reason, on a Kierkegaardian account, is no longer its own ground but is caught up in the faith-commitments of a fiduciary framework that provides for us the basic context in which we think, act, and believe.[62] Reason is constantly undergoing a "crucifixion"[63] as it is recontextualized in the "second immediacy" of faith.[64]

62. I think of a fiduciary framework as the web of commitments, practices, and language that makes it possible for us to think and speak meaningfully in the world and makes sense of it. They are comparable to Wittgenstein's concept of "forms of life." These "faith commitments" are always "ready-to-hand" and indispensable and can no more be avoided by a cognitively functioning human being than breathing by a living one. This is why Kierkegaard pits faith and doubt against each other as opposites. It is not to say that faith deals only in certainties (objective or subjective). Kierkegaard expressly avows that faith exists precisely in the presence of objective uncertainties.

63. Climacus uses the phrase "faith's crucifixion of the understanding" (Kierkegaard, *Concluding Unscientific Postscript to Philosophical Fragments*, 1.564) to suggest that the economy of reason-giving to justify beliefs is constantly supplemented by and caught up into that which is beyond its control or mastery (faith).

64. Faith is described by Kierkegaard (under the pseudonym Johannes de Silentio) as "a later immediacy" or a kind of spontaneity "after" rational deliberation. He also calls faith "the new immediacy" that cannot be canceled out by reason without thereby destroying one's self. His point is that my beliefs lose their psychological directness when I rationally reflect on their contents—in a move that may be described

If we are to follow through with this paradigm shift, we will need different metaphors to guide us as we think about the discourse of Christian faith. The goal, as I noted, is not to possess the truth for oneself in a promethean act of self-possession, but to *be in* the truth—be possessed by it, not to possess it for ourselves. In his book *Orthodoxy*, Chesterton describes his reason for accepting Christian belief as related not to its truths per se—its ability to say objectively true things about the universe—but to his experience of the Christian faith as "a truth-telling thing."[65] The truth in the surprising and seemingly unreasonable descriptions of reality that come from Christianity ("orthodoxy") is in the quality of life they elicit. Kierkegaard might say instead that the reason I am a Christian is that I am *edified* or built up by it.[66] This type of edification, or upbuilding, is deeply connected to hermeneutics as the

as canceling out their primitive immediacy. That is, rational reflection interferes with my ability to hold a belief directly. Initially, reason appears juxtaposed with my beliefs as that which constantly threatens to cancel them out by examining them to see if they are false. I can then only have beliefs by succumbing to reason and letting it first determine for me what to believe. But in faith, reason is recontextualized or suspended so that belief becomes immediately (or directly) available *once again* to the believer. The "suspension" of reason by faith, however, does not straightforwardly mean that reason is *surpassed* by faith as much as it is *suspended* or continually *delayed*—that is, it is always "over" and not simply occurring at the end of a cognitive process. Søren Kierkegaard, *Fear and Trembling* ed. and trans. Howard V. Hong and Edna H. Hong (Princeton: Princeton University Press, 1983), 82. John Milbank makes this point about the relation of reason to the ethical in de Silentio's thought, and my discussion mirrors his. The suspension of reason by faith supports reason from above (that is, *suspends* it) as the condition of its possibility. That is to say, reason's delay in faith is a purely transcendental one that does not do away with reason, but simultaneously disestablishes reason in its secular form as its own ultimate ground and reestablishes it within a new context that cannot be grounded outside of faith-commitments. Milbank, "The Sublime in Kierkegaard," in *Post-Secular Philosophy: Between Philosophy and Theology*, ed. Phillip Blond (New York: Routledge, 1998), 75. See also Kierkegaard, *Concluding Unscientific Postscript*, 1.347. Paul Ricoeur discusses a similar view in terms of the relation of rational hermeneutical reflection to belief. Ricoeur distinguishes between "a primitive naiveté" in which we accept the symbolic contents of consciousness directly and "a second naiveté" that comes "in and through [rational] criticism" and makes interpretation and belief in the contents of consciousness available to us once again. *Symbolism of Evil*, 351–52.

65. G. K. Chesterton, *Orthodoxy*, 156–57.
66. As the pastor-friend of the pseudonymous Judge William notes, "only the truth that builds up is truth for you." Søren Kierkegaard, *Either/Or*, part 2, ed. and trans. Edna H. Hong and Howard V. Hong (Princeton: Princeton University Press, 1987), 354.

motivation or goal of understanding. Rather than seeking *knowledge* in order to control, dominate, and master reality, in a hermeneutical paradigm I seek to *understand* so I may be rightly (in a right way) or be a good person or have a meaningful life—in short, that I may be or have a *self*. To rephrase Chesterton's point, the reason I accept Christian faith, then, is it enables me to interpret my life fruitfully and the world meaningfully through the practices, categories, and language of Christian faith, so that I have a more authentic understanding of myself and a sense of wholeness to my life.

I have tried to redescribe modern apologetics in a way that makes sense of my earlier double claim, first, that apologetics is a very serious *threat* to Christian faith and, second, that defending actual Christianity is, in a sense, *impossible* in modernity. I did this by describing modern apologetics so it is clear the modern epistemological paradigm, which underwrites modern apologetics, is just *one way* of telling the story about reason and belief. Furthermore, I tried to make it obvious that when apologetics accepts the modern paradigm, it places Christian belief in service to ideology and fashions for itself an idolatrous, graven image. Subsequently, modern Christian thought slowly deteriorates and suffers from what Carl Raschke describes as an "autoimmune disease." In the name of defending the faith by attacking the so-called enemies of faith, modern apologetics really attacks Christian faith itself, subverting its own legitimacy.[67]

In chapter 3 I look at the question of how we can think and talk about God, after modernity, in a way that places edification at the center of our inquiry. In doing so, I explore the question of how we may believe and witness to Christian truth in a postmodern situation that is keenly aware of human finitude and fallibility and the fragility of faith. In particular, I pursue the connection made here between hermeneutics and edification, and I attempt to reorient the task of Christian apologetics around this notion. By my account, edification is of fundamental importance to the Christian concept of witness.

---

67. Raschke, *Next Reformation*, 45.

3

Irony, Witness, and the Ethics of Belief

> Irony is a healthiness insofar as it rescues the soul from
> the snares of relativity; it is a sickness insofar as it cannot
> bear the absolute except in the form of nothing.
>
> Søren Kierkegaard

John is a self-described atheist-Roman Catholic. He earned a PhD in philosophy at an Ivy League university and is a philosophy professor at a small, prestigious college in the United States. We met several years ago at a research center, and I noticed a deep spiritual hunger in him. John was fascinated by my faith and confided in me that although he felt he no longer had faith, he nevertheless experienced this as a profound loss. John confessed that he desperately wished he could believe in God again and had even spent time in two different monasteries hoping to reignite his faith or find some deeper spiritual reality in which he could believe.

During our second week at the center, John and I were joined by two graduate students from a nearby seminary who had come to research for their master's theses. Our new friends informed John and me that they had just completed a modular course on Christian apologetics with one of the leading contemporary apologists. Jokingly, they related how the apologist described himself as "the hired gun" who rode into town to shoot down the bad guys (atheists) and their arguments and make the streets safe again for Christians.

It did not take our budding apologists long to clue in to the fact that John was not a professing Christian. And despite John's protestations that he was not interested in arguing about faith, what he did or did not believe, or how far his beliefs were or were not justified, our two apologists went to work. They took aim and started to shoot holes in the reasonableness of John's beliefs with their shiny, new apologetic six-guns.

John objected to this treatment. What bothered him, he said, was the impersonal way both he and his beliefs were being treated—as if they were abstract entities (like propositions) instead of reflections of spiritual realities with which he personally struggled. John told the apologists he found what they were doing offensive. Undaunted, our defenders of the faith assumed the apologetic right-of-way and continued with their inquisition in the name of unloading their responsibility for John's errors into God's hands—informing John at one point that it was necessary so that his "blood would not be on their heads" (actually citing Ezek. 3:18).[1] Needless to say, this did not make a positive impression and did nothing to *show* John the truth of Christianity.

Stories like John's reinforce for me that, typically, we do not come to belief by dint of mere rational persuasion. The reasons I have faith—or any other belief—and that it appears acceptable to me have to be put in the context of my lived experience and all the various construals of the world, myself, God, others, and so on. I have to accept my faith in order to feel at home with it.[2] The context in which we accept beliefs

1. In Ezek. 3:18 God says to Ezekiel, "If I say to the wicked, 'You shall surely die,' and you give them no warning, or speak to warn the wicked from their wicked way, in order to save their life, those wicked persons shall die for their iniquity; but their blood I will require at your hand."

2. We find support for this in the most unlikely of places. Alvin Plantinga's phenomenology of belief formation hinges on what he calls "impulsional evidence." See Alvin Plantinga, *Warrant and Proper Function* (New York: Oxford University Press, 1992), 192–93. Plantinga claims that we form beliefs because, at bottom, we accept them; and we accept beliefs because they have a felt attractiveness to us. That is, they present us with an "impulse" to believe them: we only accept those beliefs that

(or have faith) are varied, personal, and rarely fall under our direct, conscious, rational control. And I hazard to say we collectively experience in our spiritual lives the same "breach of naïveté," as Charles Taylor might say, that makes faith difficult for John. This is yet another symptom of our condition of secularity that exposes faith and makes it vulnerable from a number of directions—not just to objections of rational coherence. In a secular age, faith is susceptible to what we might call issues of existential coherence. This means that even when we affirm and believe identical creedal confessions, we do so in a manner different from premodern affirmations of them.[3] We have lost, as it were, the naïveté—or immediacy or directness—of belief, in God due to a massive shift in the overall context in which we seek to interpret our lives and understand the world. As a result, there is a fragility that characterizes faith today.[4] *Having* faith, believing for oneself, must be understood not only in reference to our being able to establish the reasonableness of belief but also in terms of how it fits with our lived experience and the sense we make of the world.

When we operate from the perspective of the modern epistemological paradigm, we mostly ignore the extent to which having faith is tied to the often-unacknowledged background values, assumptions, and practices that give shape to our perspective and meaning to our lives. Instead, we tend to focus only on the objective, neutral, and universal reasons that may or may not justify belief. In this way John's story shows us (albeit in a rather exaggerated way) how far modern apologetics drifts from the way I want to think about the Christian concept of witness. Of course, not all apologists think and act like the two who confronted

---

seem to us to be true. When we consider the alternatives, they do not have the same attractiveness to us—they "feel" different. For example, Plantinga says, we typically believe 2 + 1 = 3 because it *feels right*, and not because we possess any propositional or sensory evidence for this. The alternatives—say, 2 + 1 = 7—just feel "wrong, weird, absurd, eminently rejectable." Alvin Plantinga, "Respondeo Ad Feldman," in *Warrant in Contemporary Epistemology: Essays in Honor of Plantinga's Theory of Knowledge*, ed. Jonothan L. Kvanvig (London: Rowman and Littlefield, 1996), 259.

3. Charles Taylor, *A Secular Age* (Cambridge, MA: Belknap, 2007), 13.

4. The "fragility of faith" is David Wisdo's phrase in Wisdo, *The Life of Irony and the Ethics of Belief* (New York: State University of New York Press, 1993), 87ff. My understanding of the fragility of faith has some congruence with Wisdo's, but also differs sharply at key points.

John.[5] But whatever else Christian apologetics is, it must, at very least, involve witnessing to the truth of Christian belief. Thus, I suggest in this chapter we move the metaphors we use to characterize the Christian witness away from those used by modern apologetics.

What concerns me most in John's story is that the actions of the two seminarians are entirely consistent with the modern apologetic paradigm taken in its own right.[6] Their overriding concern is not with John's *edification*—that is, his personal building up as a self before God—but with the *epistemological justification* of his beliefs. When—as in the modern epistemological paradigm—the truth of the gospel is construed solely in objective terms, as contained in propositions, doctrines, and intellectual positions, and when the rationality of belief is regarded as of primary importance in legitimizing faith, the main issue on which a witness will focus is the reasonableness of a nonbeliever's beliefs, positions, or worldview. A person's subjective and personal interests and concerns, as well as the wider set of factors that impinge on a person's ability to believe or disbelieve, are largely irrelevant to the primary activity of apologetics. Instead, these are in fact the very influences on belief that must be *overcome* or *ignored* so that belief may be held in a fully rational way.

Apostles and Apologetics

If we understand the essence of Christianity as *edification*, not objectively in terms of propositions, and if we place *it* (edification) at the

5. Unfortunately, a frightening number of Christians do seem to behave this way when "defending the faith." The evidence is anecdotal but telling. One personal testimony of this sort is that of Randall "Peg" Peters, who recounts how he put his formal training in apologetics to work at university, debating for an entire year with his atheist friend, Steve. At the end of eight months Steve could no longer refute or rebut any of Peg's arguments—yet he still refused to accept Christianity. In exasperation Peg asked why Steve would not become a Christian, and Steve's response was, "I don't really want to end up like you!" Randall "Peg" Peters, Dave Phillips, and Quentin Steen, *The Colours of God: Toward an Emerging Theology* (Bloomington, IN: Xlibris, 2008), 31.

6. It is true that a faith completely informed by Scripture will be able to note inconsistencies between the gospel and the actions of these two seminarians, even if one accepts the modern paradigm. My point, however, is that modern apologetics needs an impulse from outside its paradigm to check it.

center of our witness instead of epistemic justification, a question naturally arises. How would John's two apologists behave if they were first-century apostles of Jesus? Would they—or *could* they—believe, act, and write as they currently do in defense of Christianity?[7] Will someone who believes they have heard God speak bother to make clever arguments, brilliantly piecing together the evidence, so that the rational inescapability of the message is shown to be universally, objectively, and neutrally justified?[8] Will this individual even feel the need to *show* Christianity is true in an objective, rational way?

It should be clear the question here is not whether a particular apologist professes to believe a message really is from God, nor is it whether one can genuinely be a Christian and engage in modern apologetics. It is not even a matter of the reasonability of Christian beliefs, or whether a believer might be able to point to evidence or arguments that support their beliefs. The deeper issue here is the appropriateness of even attempting a modern apologetic. The point I make in the previous chapters is that when modern apologetics endeavors to justify itself using the tools, assumptions, and methods of modern philosophy, it does so in terms of interests that are foreign—and even hostile—to Christian faith. So my question is whether a rational apologetics can serve as "spiritual medicine" for a culture filled with people like John who are spiritually impoverished by the secularity of our modern condition.[9] The truth of Christianity obviously has a large bearing on our spiritual health, but I cannot see how the same can be said for our being able to *show* it objectively in a manner prescribed by the modern epistemological paradigm.

There is a great deal more to be said on the subject of a rational (modern) apologetics, but this is sufficient to set the stage for me to

7. Cf. Merold Westphal, *Kierkegaard's Critique of Reason and Society* (University Park, PA: Pennsylvania State University Press, 1991), 10–13, in which he sets up a similar scenario, with a parallel question regarding the appropriateness of a scientific philosophy of religion. My treatment of apologetics here is indebted to Westphal's exploration of the possibility of a prophetic phenomenology of religion.

8. Note that one of the central problems that modern critical scholarship has with the Gospels and the New Testament as a whole is the apparent lack of conformity to modern standards of rationality by the biblical texts, precisely in their appeals to "evidence" or to "history."

9. Cf. Westphal, *Kierkegaard's Critique of Religion and Society*, 11.

explore the possibility that the model for a Christian apologist may be someone other than an analytic philosopher, scientist, or lawyer (or some combination of all three)—all of which are different forms of genius. Using Steven Cowan's classifications once again,[10] three of his apologetic types—Classical, Reformed Epistemology, and Presuppositional—project the model-apologist as an analytic philosopher who is able to exploit the latest philosophical theories and scientific conclusions in defense of Christianity. Evidential Apologetics models the apologist after a scientist or philosopher-scientist who gathers evidence and draws conclusions. And Cumulative Case Apologetics works with the model of the apologist as a kind of lawyer who is able to invoke expert testimony from philosophers, scientists, and other experts to make a persuasive case. We could also add to these a "professional journalist" model of apologetics, in which the apologist interviews and examines a series of expert sources for their testimony.[11] In any case, what we have across the board is the *professionalization of Christian witness*. Each of these apologetic models depends on skills and abilities that only a few "brilliant" Christian thinkers possess. And so the rest of us require books, seminars, and courses in apologetics written and taught by the professionals (geniuses, experts) who can equip us with the appropriate apologetic tools and weapons to "witness" to our neighbors.

This professional model of Christian apologetics and witness is an aspect of the modern apologetic paradigm I wish to leave behind, because it is an integral part of what traps us in the incipient nihilism of modernity. It seems to inspire exactly the sort of apologetic confrontation John had to endure. Instead, I want to pattern our apologetic efforts after apostles who do not ground their message in their own genius but in a transcendent word from God. This will mean apologetic discourse is first and foremost *prophetic*. The basic form of apostolic speech is kerygmatic—from the New Testament

10. Steven B. Cowan, ed., *Five Views on Apologetics* (Grand Rapids: Zondervan, 2000).

11. See Lee Strobel, *The Case for Christ: A Journalist's Personal Investigation of the Evidence for Jesus* (Grand Rapids: Zondervan, 1998). Perhaps not surprisingly, Strobel was educated in law at Yale Law School. Since the spectacular success of this book, Strobel has gone on to write an entire series of "The Case for . . ." (Faith, Easter, a Creator) apologetics books.

Greek word, *kerygma*, for "proclamation" or "preaching"—for apostles are those who have been sent on a mission with a message. The apostle's primary discourse is addressed to particular people as individual selves—to build up, exhort, encourage, rebuke, reprove, reform, instruct, enrich, enlighten, and reassure them. The apostle is not appealing to theoretical reason as the ground or basis on which the message should be accepted. Apostles and prophets present their message in the form of an exhortation: "Hear the word of the Lord!" They ask people to accept their message because it comes from God and not because it is a piece of clever analysis or because they are specially qualified.[12]

To be clear, while I am suggesting a postmodern witness should be grounded in *kerygma* (proclamation or announcement of the Christian gospel), I'm not suggesting it is ever reducible to it—except to the degree any proper *kerygma* is thoroughly immersed in the culture in which it is proclaimed (its conceptual categories, concerns, practices, modes of address, etc.). There will always be more in *kerygma* than witness, and apologetics or witness will necessarily take us to different places than those reached through mere proclamation—most notably into dialogue with others. When I witness, I do not take up a self-centered, asymmetrical stance closed off to the needs, wants, desires, goals, dreams, story, or insights of the person to whom I witness.[13] That is to say, witness is not a monologue but is dialogical in nature. Precisely in faithfulness to Christ and to the truth to which I witness, I must be open to others when I witness. To be sure, witness involves taking a stand on what I believe and making a commitment to the place I occupy. But witness is inherently social. It involves *listening* to others, as well as speaking, and it involves *being with* others. It requires what Miroslav Volf calls a "catholic personality," whose identity is

12. I have argued that a postmodern apologetic should be grounded in *kerygma* in "Postmodern Apologetics," in *A New Kind of Conversation: Blogging Toward a Postmodern Faith*, ed. Myron Bradley Penner and Hunter Barnes (Colorado Springs: Authentic, 2007), 137–42. James K. A. Smith also argues that a postmodern apologetics must be grounded in proclamation (*kerygma*), not demonstration. *Who's Afraid of Postmodernism? Taking Derrida, Lyotard, and Foucault to Church* (Grand Rapids: Baker Academic, 2006), 28.

13. Cf. David K. Clark, *Dialogical Apologetics: A Person-Centered Approach* (Grand Rapids: Baker, 1993), 116–17.

always *with others* precisely because it is shaped by the gospel and engaged in the transformation of the world.[14]

Thus in witness, as I engage in dialogue with others, I speak and understand God's Word differently because of my personal interaction with them.[15] But witnesses are not necessarily people who understand their confession in all its theoretical details and rational implications. What is of primary importance is that the witness *believes* it and is *committed* to understanding it, and in that commitment is edified in all the ways truth edifies others. To say it differently, prophetic witness is good hermeneutical practice and is crucial to making an interpretive tradition a living one.[16]

The Ethics of Belief

We may begin by noting that witness, as a species of prophetic speech, is personal.[17] Prophets and apostles do not speak in terms of abstract universals but directly address *persons*. According to Gerhard van Rad, God meets the Hebrew prophet in his Word in the most personal way possible, and this means the prophet cannot treat it as if it were a

14. Miroslav Volf, *Exclusion and Embrace: A Theological Exploration of Identity, Otherness, and Reconciliation* (Nashville: Abingdon, 1996), 51–55. In Miroslav Volf, *After Our Likeness: The Church as the Image of Trinity* (Grand Rapids: Eerdmans, 1998), 278, Volf makes it clear that the "catholicity" or openness of the Christian is connected to our identity (1) with the church, which (2) is grounded in God's very life as Trinity.

15. Here is where I come closest to agreeing with William Lane Craig on apologetics, when he warns against skipping past the straightforward declaration of what one believes and moving straight to the apologetic task of philosophical argumentation. But this also highlights where I disagree most profoundly with him, because Craig wishes to couch all of this in terms of what is rational for both the Christian believer and the unbeliever to accept as true.

16. Richard Bauckham, *Bible and Mission: Christian Witness in a Postmodern World* (Grand Rapids: Baker Academic, 2003), makes a similar argument for the importance of "witness" as the paradigm for postmodern mission. Bauckham argues that witness is the form of assertion most appropriate to the nature of Christian truth in postmodernity. It is "an extremely valuable image with which to meet the postmodern suspicion of all metanarratives as oppressive" (99). I am in full agreement. His proposal has a different focus than mine but provides an extremely valuable sketch of a hermeneutical framework centered on a concept of biblical narrative that connects Christian witness to mission.

17. Westphal, *Kierkegaard's Critique of Reason and Society*, 12–14.

neutral or abstract thing.[18] Prophets receive their message personally and directly. Therefore, they are not able to take a logical, rational stance toward it and do not waste a lot of time or energy arguing with their audience about whether their message is rationally justified. Merold Westphal observes that, in this kind of speech, monotheism or belief in God is not a theoretical hypothesis put forward for debate or discussion. We might say belief in God is assumed as part of the language game of prophetic speech, and without that assumption the prophet's message cannot make any sense at all.[19] Not surprisingly, then, prophetic speech is delivered as *the* Word of the Lord, not *a* word.[20] It is what God intends for *these* people in *this* concrete situation—at this particular time, with this history, these problems, etc.—and so is the only word that matters! The driving concern of prophetic speech is the edification of *this* particular person or people, and edification is the controlling interest that overrides any anxieties over the rational justification of the message or its conformity to the canons of logic and science.

Thus, the form of argumentation in prophetic speech—if indeed arguments are provided—is most often markedly *ad hominem*. That is, it appeals to characteristics unique to the person; it literally argues "to the person" whose mind is to be changed, as much as it undermines the rational justification for believing and acting as the person does.[21] Prophets do this because they address humans on behalf of God. "Thus," as Westphal explains, "it never occurs to prophets to present their message in the mode of universally valid truths and imperatives."[22] As an example, he points to the Hebrew prophet Amos, who does not produce a formally valid, or even inductively cogent, argument

18. Gerhard von Rad, *Old Testament Theology*, trans. D. M. G. Stalker (New York: Harper & Row, 1962–1965), 2:89. Westphal uses this citation in *Kierkegaard's Critique of Reason and Society*, 12.

19. Wittgenstein makes a similar point: "Imagine a language-game 'When I call you, come in through the door.' In any ordinary case, a doubt whether there really is a door there will be impossible." Ludwig Wittgenstein, *On Certainty*, ed. G. E. M. Anscombe and G. H. von Wright, trans. Denis Paul and G. E. M. Anscombe (San Francisco: Harper Torchbooks, 1969), §391.

20. Cf. Westphal, *Kierkegaard's Critique of Reason and Society*, 12.

21. Ibid., 13–14.

22. Ibid., 12.

that uses objectively agreed upon premises for his conclusion that the
Hebrew God is faithful; nor does Amos infer from reasons that are
objective, universal, and neutral the imperative for God's people to
be faithful to their God. Rather Amos declares:

> Seek good, and not evil,
>   that you may live;
> and so the LORD, the God of hosts, will be with you,
>   as you have said.
>
> Amos 5:14 (ESV)

A crucial underpinning of Amos's speech is his audience's (Israel's) confession of Yahweh as their God and themselves as Yahweh's
people. But he is not at all offering them an argument whose form
and evidential basis yield a timelessly and universally true conclusion.
It is a conditional truth.[23] One response to Amos from his hearers
might be something like, "Well, we made a mistake! We now understand things better and no longer believe that." In fact, Westphal
notes, the conditional truths expressed in the message of prophets
like Amos—and even more so, Jonah—are often of the sort that
can be falsified by us if we change our behavior.[24] What is critical in
Amos's speech is that he takes his audience seriously in terms of their
personal commitments, and his appeal to them is centered on what
will build them up in those commitments—what we might call their
project.

23. Conditional truths, it can be argued, may still be absolutely true insofar as
they express what will happen necessarily if certain conditions are obtained. To
begin with, I have trouble with the correspondence theory of truth that forces us
to make an argument like this. However, even assuming a correspondence theory, I
still insist that the central preoccupation of the prophet is not with elucidating the
rational conditions for timeless truths but in calling God's people back to faithful
relationship with God. And the fact that prophets do this using human language and
thought forms that include various kinds of arguments should not confuse the issue.
Prophets will abandon any form of discourse that jeopardizes their more important
goal of proclaiming God's Word and calling people to be faithful to that Word. They
are not put off if they cannot respond to the latest, most sophisticated philosophical and scientific objections to their message. I suspect they will instead view those
objections as simply one more form of unfaithfulness.

24. Westphal, *Kierkegaard's Critique of Reason and Society*, 13–14.

When couched in terms of prophetic speech and edification, it becomes apparent that one of the methodological sins of modernity is its objectification of persons. The focus of modern apologetics is on epistemic justification of belief as the apologetic bottom-line rather than on the personal edification of those whom we encounter. In the case of modern apologetics, our concern is with the objective relation between an individual as a certain kind of object in the world and other objects in the world (such as propositions and their relation between the "thinking things" that believe them and the other things to which they refer).[25] But the unbeliever is not essentially a *mind* that happens to have a body—a "thing that thinks"[26] whose *telos* (end or goal) is fulfilled when it contemplates or acknowledges the correct propositions. Rather, humans are embodied *persons* who find their fulfillment in becoming a self that is in proper relation to itself, others, and the world. And this, Christianity teaches, can only happen if the self is first in proper relation to God. If this is the case, then *how* one arrives at belief and maintains it is as important as *what* one believes.[27] As Aristotle (and the entire aretaic tradition) notes, if one is accidentally good, one is not thereby virtuous. The same is true of the cognitive contents of our beliefs: when they are objectively true, one is not thereby *in* the truth. Thus, the apostle James declares that if it were a mere matter of believing the right objective propositions about God, then the demons are much more suitable candidates for salvation than humans.

To put it another way, when we take prophetic speech as the basis for apologetic witness, we move from an abstract epistemology of belief to an ethics of belief. When I speak of an *ethics* of belief, I mean a focus not just on *what* one believes but also on *how* one believes. It is a practical question about the personal values and cares we have and the practices which they inform and out of which they emerge. Ethics in this sense does not begin abstractly with theory but is concerned

25. Kierkegaard describes this kind of objectification as a focus on the "what" of belief rather than on the "how."

26. This is, of course, a reference to Descartes's "substance dualist" view of the human being. See René Descartes, *Discourse on Method* and *Meditations on First Philosophy*, 3rd ed., trans. Donald A. Cress (Indianapolis: Hackett, 1993), 59.

27. Note that I am *not* saying that what one believes is unimportant.

with our concrete modes of being who we are: our actions—what Kierkegaard refers to as *actuality*. An ethics of belief, then, first and foremost refers to a concern with persons as *subjects* who *are*. Rather than the abstract, theoretical categories of epistemology, a person's subjectivity or personhood, one's being as a subject, is the starting place for reflection on beliefs.[28] As I already suggested, what our age needs is not a scientific or theoretical answer to intellectual challenges of belief but a personal response to the spiritual problems of people who have been unable to receive and have faith. This response, of course, must be Christian lives shaped by biblical and theological categories, and articulated responsibly with intellectual acumen and philosophical sophistication. But we need to understand the beliefs that shape Christian lives and stories in terms of norms that govern our actions in the actual contexts in which we perform them. Ethics, in other words, is the category of edification, and an ethics of belief has the same concerns as prophetic speech—concrete particularity and personal transformation.

This kind of ethics of belief is carried out by Gabriel Marcel in *Creative Fidelity*, where he speaks about "incarnate being" and "belonging and disposability" (*disponibilité*)[29] in order to fashion an approach to believing and human being that counteracts the objectivism of abstract modern epistemological categories. For Marcel, to be human is to be "incarnated." He describes this as appearing "to oneself as body, as this particular body, without being identified with it nor distinguished from it."[30] According to Marcel, the modern epistemological paradigm forces us to *dis*incarnate human being. This happens when I treat myself as an object that is essentially absent from my body (as "a thing that thinks"). When I do this, Marcel notes, I depersonalize and dehumanize the world—and I even

28. This is not to privilege practice over theory and continue to play them off each other as in the modern paradigm. It is rather to note that the place from which we theorize is always within and about and toward our concrete practices.

29. The French term *disponibilité* is translated here as "disposability" but may also be translated as "availability" or even "handiness." The way Marcel uses the term signals a *spiritual* availability or openness to the other and a readiness to respond. Cf. the translator's note in Marcel, *Creative Fidelity*, trans. Robert Rosthal (New York: The Noonday Press, 1964), 57n1.

30. Marcel, *Creative Fidelity*, 20.

depersonalize my own self. The spiritual being of a person is never disconnected from time and place. People—individual persons— have bodies that take up space, require nourishment, get hurt, and are stimulated in innumerable ways. Bodies act as the location in which, and means by which, the world is experienced and our lives are lived. A person has a context, and a body is more than the sum of its biological processes.

In addition to ourselves and the world around us, we treat *other persons* as though they were essentially absent from their bodies. We think and act as though others were *things* that belong to us and are at our disposal. To abstract or distinguish persons from what we may call their ensouled bodies is an illusion, Marcel warns, and is not how we "naturally" encounter them. We learn it from the modern scientific pursuit of objective truth, which splits us off from material reality in order to study and know it (empirically, epistemologically). Marcel describes this abstract, scientific pursuit of reality as having a hypnotic effect that renders its arbitrary and idolatrous character invisible to us—we do not notice that this scientific objectivism has conferred being on *itself* and has unnaturally riven human being into mind and body.[31]

This scientific, epistemological posture focuses on others as *objects* or bodies, and the result is that others become objects that exist *for me* (to know, to study). In doing this, I treat another individual as a "him" or "her" whose self is essentially absent, rather than an other "I" whose self or person is fully present.[32] That is, when I engage reality from a scientific, epistemological posture, I treat you as if you belong to me. And when I treat you this way, "*you belong to me* means *you are my thing*; I will dispose of you as I want."[33] Marcel therefore urges us to move from a posture of "you belong to me" and I can dispose of you as I choose, to "I belong to you" and *I* am at *your* disposal.[34] To *believe* someone, then, is "to give, or better yet, open a credit account to someone," so that belief changes *how* I am in the world and

31. Ibid., 30.
32. Ibid., 32–33. The text uses the term "Thou" instead of "I" to indicate the personal and full presence of an other self.
33. Ibid., 40.
34. Ibid.

even *who* I am.[35] And the credit I extend to someone is, he explains, *myself*. In belief "I lend myself" to the other person, not in a way that binds me to the other person, but in such a way that indicates how I intend to be toward that person, "my position with respect to [them]," or the starting point for my relationship to that person. My beliefs, then, are connected not to an abstract, theoretical position I occupy cognitively but to who I am, how I comport myself in the world, and, even more, how I relate to other persons.

If Christianity is a *way*—of life, of *being in the truth* in this world—with practices that give shape to its beliefs and beliefs that give expression to its practices, it should come as no surprise that we cannot begin abstractly and objectively and still hope to capture the essence of Christianity. Christianity must be incarnated. Actual Christianity means *being Christian* in specific ways: trusting, praying, believing, loving, witnessing. And rather than an objective event that is reducible to the cognitive acceptance of propositions, being a Christian is personal in Marcel's sense. It involves personally encountering God in Jesus Christ (a person) and being in a relationship with God-in-Jesus that changes us and everything else. If this is true, William Lane Craig's distinction between knowing Christianity and showing it to be true evaporates. A rational and objective apologetic cannot *show* or *demonstrate* these subjective realities of Christian faith. What is needed in our witness, if those we engage are to be edified, is a *poetics* that *performs* the essentially Christian,[36] in which there is no gap between the form of witness and its content. We do not need a philosophical argument that rationally justifies the objective content of Christian belief to show us it is edifying. Another irony, of course, in Craig's testimony is his open acknowledgment that genuine Christianity was shown to him powerfully and convincingly, without arguments or evidence, through the lives of those who witnessed to him.

When I refer to the subjective realities of faith, I do not mean Christianity has nothing of what we might call an objective reality

35. Ibid., 134.
36. Poetics, in the Kierkegaardian sense that I use it here, refers to the reconciliation of what is actually the case to its ideal. Poetics appeals to the imagination to perform this reconciliation. See Joel D. S. Rasmussen, *Between Irony and Witness: Kierkegaard's Poetics of Faith, Hope, and Love* (New York: T&T Clark, 2005), 10–11.

apart from its subjective appropriation—as if we might, as Cyril Connolly reportedly said, merely select the illusion that appeals best to our temperament and embrace it with passion. A worry of this sort turns on a particular understanding of the terms "objectivity" and "subjectivity." As I see it, however, the best way to understand the concepts of "objectivity" and "subjectivity" is to view them as referring to two *styles* of thinking.[37] Objectivity thinks of the world in terms of objects and how things stand in relation to other objects, while subjectivity thinks of—or, better, *relates to*—the world in terms of subjects and their relation to the world as subjects. My claim is that when I relate to the world as a subject, I presuppose something outside of myself to which I relate. That is to say, I assume there is a kind of objectivity that is appropriate for me. But if I relate to the world in a completely objective way, I need not suppose there is anything subjective about the world at all. And the more I am objective, the less subjectivity can even appear on my horizon. So when I say that *actual* Christian faith or the essentially Christian is a matter of subjectivity, I am not saying Christian faith is whatever one wants it to be or that it is absolutely relative and arbitrary. Rather, I am trying to point out that when one approaches faith through subjectivity or as a subject—that is, when I think and speak of faith in terms of what it means for *me* to *have* and *exercise* faith—then the appropriate "objectivity" of faith, or its transpersonal dimension or the fact that I have not made it all up, is just assumed. What is more, I lose the subjectivity of faith and its subject-building character (as edifying) the more I attempt to understand it as a merely objective thing.

My point is this: If our approach to Christian belief is not to remain lost in epistemological abstraction and objectivity, and if we are to find a prophetic model of witness that will be able to come forth as *edification*[38]—as a spiritual activity that is itself an expression of faith—then our account of Christian belief will need to be couched in terms of an ethics of belief and not just an epistemology.

37. Cf. David Wisdo's account of Max Deuser's position on "subjecting" and "objecting" in Wisdo, *Ethics of Belief*, 130–31.
38. This is a play on the title of Merold Westphal's essay, "Prolegomena to Any Future Philosophy of Religion That Will Be Able to Come Forth as Prophecy," in Westphal, *Kierkegaard's Critique of Reason and Society*, 1–27.

Irony and In/Direct Witness

All of this brings us to a second feature of prophetic speech. In addition to being personal, prophetic speech is *ironic*. Apostles and prophets are deeply suspicious of the meaning-making strategies we employ and the structures for legitimating and justifying beliefs in our dominant social structures. Irony generally involves an incongruity between how we act in, talk about, or think about a situation and the usual expectations for that situation—between what is formally presented in a statement or situation and what is obviously true about it. When we think of it in a deeper sense, though, irony is a subtle form of protest against our social conventions for (pre)establishing meaning and rules for what one can or cannot say, mean, or do in a given situation. It communicates something against the given rules and in spite of them. As a rough definition, then, we could say irony is the art of exploiting—either in speech or other forms of action—the agreed upon "rules" for rational discourse in order to highlight their failure to capture things as they really are.[39] Irony inserts itself into the gap between our thoughts and reality, our words and the truth, the way we refer to things and the way they *really are*. And when we use it, irony places us and those with whom we discourse in the middle of that gap, leaving us with a choice about what to make of it all. So when I speak or act ironically, I create an ambiguity—or what we may call a negative space—for my audience, which gives them a kind of freedom. My ironic words or actions create a situation in which the social and rational expectations are undermined or questioned so that at some level the audience has a choice to make about how they will understand me.

When an apostle or prophet declares they have a message from God to me, it is a form of address that leaves me free with respect to what I understand them to really be saying and also to appropriate

39. Thus, Søren Kierkegaard provides us with a good example when he explains that "the ironic to the first power lies in the erection of a kind of epistemology that annihilates itself; the ironic to the second power lies in Socrates's pretending [in Plato's *The Republic*] that by accident he found himself defending Protagoras's thesis, although he in fact crushes it by the defense itself." *The Concept of Irony with Continual Reference to Socrates*, ed. and trans. Howard V. Hong and Edna H. Hong (Princeton: Princeton University Press, 1989), 61.

(or not) what I understand in the message. There are two key features of this irony in prophetic Christian witness within modernity. First, we have already noted the impossibility of defending Christianity in modernity. In as much as we wish to make Christianity appear *plausible* by modern standards, we lose its character as the essential action of a life of faith with and before God. Genuinely prophetic speech is ironic because it does not attempt to ameliorate or soften the rational scandal of its message. It does not first justify itself or its message according to the standards of human reason. In other words, prophetic speech preserves the paradox of faith.

It is perhaps easy to overlook the second ironic feature of prophetic witness, because when apostles and prophets deliver their message, it comes to us in a deceptively straightforward manner: this person or these people are addressed directly with a message that says, "Repent!" or "This is the way; walk in it!" or something of the sort. But in reflecting on prophetic speech, one must take careful note of the nature of the prophetic speech-act. As we mentioned in the previous chapter, apostles or prophets are not speaking on their own and delivering messages they take responsibility for; they are speaking on behalf of God and by God's power or Spirit. The message is not theirs (alone) but is first and foremost *from God*. So while it may appear that prophets speak directly, there is deceptiveness or irony to this, for they do not ground the truth of their message in their own adequacy to discover or understand it, nor even to utter it. The irony of this is in the claim to speak the truth while having no direct access to the ground or source of its truthfulness. God provides the grounds for both the prophetic word and its delivery, and it is the call of God that makes apostles or prophets adequate to their mission and their message. Prophetic irony disavows all human attempts to justify the message while maintaining its authority over us and its ability to speak truly to us. The form of the message—its human messenger—belies prophetic speech as an authoritative word from God.

The sense in which prophets are ironic, then, deepens our concept of irony, for here irony is not just a literary device. Prophets sometimes use irony in their speeches, but not very often. The sense in which they are ironic is more of a *stance* or a way of being that indicates a particular kind of relationship between themselves, their persons, and their words (that is, the *ground* of their discourse). When prophets speak God's word, speak *for* God, they do so in a way that does not appeal to accepted norms for legitimation. Hebrew prophets usually begin by professing their own personal inadequacy to speak for God, and almost without exception they stand outside the temple (or tabernacle) cult of Israel. They (with one or two exceptions) are not priests and are not vested with religious authority by the existing religious structures—in fact, they call these structures into question and are critical of them. But it is not as if their discourse is completely *un*grounded. The prophetic appeal for authority, validation, and legitimation is simply and directly to *God*, and they leave it to their audience to work this out with God for themselves—will they listen and obey, or not?[40] Thus, the irony I am describing is not just a manner of speaking but a personal, philosophical stance in which my words (as discourse) are not inherently justified. My speech belies its ground of justification. My right to speak the way I do is neither self-grounded nor immediately obvious because of who I am or the brilliance of my discourse.

Christianly speaking, irony is a lived awareness that the "rules" of Christian speech or discourse (e.g., doctrine, creeds, councils) and the particular vision of the Christian faith of one's community are less than ultimate—that they are not God's but are instead our fashioning of what he has revealed to us. All our theologies and verbal confessions of Jesus Christ as Lord fail to encapsulate the essence of Jesus or express fully the life of faith. The irony of Christian talk about God is nicely captured by C. S. Lewis in his poem "Footnote to All Prayers," in which he insists our words always fail to express adequately who God is. Lewis begins by declaring agnostically that "He whom I bow to knows only to whom I bow," and describes *all* our words, images, and symbols for God as literal blasphemy and idolatry. He closes the poem, pleading with God, "Take not, O Lord, our literal sense. Lord, in Thy great, / Unbroken speech our limping metaphor translate."[41]

40. Many prophets are not recognized as such in their own lifetime and are often persecuted and even killed. Interestingly, it is the children of those who killed and persecuted the prophets in Israel who recognize that they did in fact speak for God— that their message, while "illegitimate," was the truth and was edifying and faithful.

41. Another part of the poem states, "And all men in their praying, self-deceived, address / The coinage of their own unquiet thoughts, unless / Thou in magnetic mercy to Thyself divert / Our arrows, aimed unskillfully, beyond desert; / And all men are

You see, Lewis is enough of an ironist to understand that we cannot equate our speech about God with the being of God. Instead, we *appropriate* the words and creeds we receive as true because they capture us, mold and shape us, and make us true. They prove in our lives to be a "truth-telling thing," to borrow Chesterton's idiom again. This is connected to the life of faith as a kind of "second immediacy" or another naïveté,[42] for in the negative space of irony we create room (again) for the possibility of faith. In this context there is no ground for seeing faith as abstract or theoretical. To have faith is to express it in one's life—the essence of Christianity. It is, in other words, to *be* Christian.

Irony is the only way to express the kind of truth prophets wish to communicate—the kind of understanding that produces genuine *self*-understanding and expresses actual Christianity. The ironic in/directness of Christian prophetic speech finds its ultimate expression in Jesus's incarnation. As the God-man, Jesus is the "absolute paradox" whom the Scriptures describe not only as *the* Word of God but also as "the way, and the truth, and the life."[43] It is not just that Jesus speaks the words of God better and more clearly than other prophets. Christians believe Jesus *is* God's Word. In fact, the human Jesus has an "indirect identity" with God the Father that corresponds to God's indirect identity in and with his revelation.[44] This is the supreme irony, as Kierkegaard would say: that God was a human being and there were people who lived with him, spoke with him, ate with him, and heard him speak, and yet did not realize they were in the presence of God. It was possible to miss both Jesus's divine identity as well as his message, because there is a deep incongruity between Jesus's Word and words and the creaturely medium through which we encounter them. God, to put it another way, is a master ironist whose Word

idolaters, crying unheard / To a deaf idol, if Thou take them at their word" (C. S. Lewis, *Poems* [New York: Mariner, 2002], 129–30).

42. See 74n64 above.

43. John 14:6; John 1:1; cf. Heb. 1:1–3.

44. Cf. Karl Barth, *Church Dogmatics* I/1, ed. G. W. Bromiley and T. F. Torrance (Edinburgh: T&T Clark, 2004), 137. I have benefited much from John Franke's emphasis on this aspect of Barth's thought. See John R. Franke, "The Nature of Theology: Culture, Language, and Truth," in *Christianity and the Postmodern Turn: Six Views*, ed. Myron B. Penner (Grand Rapids: Brazos, 2005), 209–10.

comes to us in a form that is not directly identical to the message. In communicating God's Word—himself—to us, God leaves us free with respect to the communication. The nature of reality, the world, and God himself is such that truthful speech about them—the kind of speech that communicates what is most important—ultimately is ironic.

Irony, Edification, and Witness

Not only apostles and prophets but many postmodernists too recognize the importance of irony. They no longer take for granted that their current vocabulary is sufficient to describe and judge things as they *really are* and that they can derive a foundational set of beliefs about God or the world that are rationally inescapable. Richard Rorty thinks of irony as a hermeneutical strategy to counter the commonsense view of epistemology, which says we have direct cognitive access to the way the world actually is and our current metaphors and vocabulary are sufficient to describe the world accurately.[45] So-called common sense tells us that if on any point we are wrong, it is only because we have not tried hard enough to be clear about the world or to understand it well enough or in the right way. We need to do more research or refine our vocabulary. The way to solve the conflicts between competing descriptions of the world, then, is to get down to the facts: to translate competing vocabularies into a neutral language that captures the essence of things and provides us with a basis for comparison so we may determine the adequacy (or inadequacy) of a given vocabulary. But Rorty's ironist recognizes the radical contingency of language and human thought and so gives up on the notion that there is such a thing as neutral criteria to adjudicate between competing vocabularies.

Rorty explains that an ironist realizes anything can be made to look bad or good simply by redescribing it in an alternative vocabulary. Ironists do not, however, abandon their current vocabulary, but as they use it, they always do so with the keen awareness that it is not

45. Richard Rorty, *Contingency, Irony, and Solidarity* (Cambridge: Cambridge University Press, 1989).

ultimate. They nourish radical and abiding doubts as to its efficacy.[46] The ironist's present vocabulary is simply the best one available at the present moment. So when the ironist uses this vocabulary, the ironist fully assumes responsibility for its shortcomings and understands the vocabulary is only a provisional medium. It is therefore characteristic of Rortian ironists that they play descriptions of reality against redescriptions by imaginatively engaging alternate and new vocabularies through works of literature. But none of this is, for Rorty, anything like the pursuit of truth. Rorty, in fact, so thoroughly disconnects the object of our believing to truth that he is able to argue for the importance of saying what we believe even though it is disadvantageous to do so (his description of "truthfulness"), without tying this in any way to a conviction that what we say is true.[47] There is no hope of seeing reality as it really is, or even a desire to do so. Irony goes all the way down.

Because true speech is not possible for humans, Rorty shifts the discussion away from truth to edification.[48] Truth, for Rorty, is *made* by us rather than *found*; and it is a property of human minds, not of the world (or anything outside of the human mind to which our sentences may refer). Rorty proposes irony as the main coping strategy for our epistemic situation, in which nothing we say can be determinately true. Because he believes language is radically contingent and unable to capture the world as it really is, and truth in the sense of anything final or normative is impossible, Rorty recommends we give up talking about truth and seeking it, and instead focus on *solidarity*—fostering a plurality of perspectives and beliefs in our intellectual communities and coming to a consensus about how and what to believe. So we should not be surprised Rorty replaces the search for objective truth with an emphasis on edification and consensus. What he seems to mean is edification is a social and cultural project that has no determinative criteria or goal, except to eschew restrictive norms and to perpetually re-form and re-create oneself in the interest of being more attuned to plurality and difference. According to Rorty, irony is

46. James Conant, "Freedom, Cruelty, and Truth: Rorty Versus Orwell," in *Rorty and His Critics*, ed. Robert B. Brandom (Malden, MA: Blackwell, 2000), 258–340.

47. Richard Rorty, "Response to James Conant," in *Rorty and His Critics*, 347.

48. Richard Rorty, *Philosophy and the Mirror of Nature* (Princeton: Princeton University Press, 1979), 357.

a strategy I should employ (if I am to be a good liberal intellectual) in order to direct my thinking away from my own private purposes and toward ends that contribute to public edification or "good."

All of this should sound familiar, for it is strikingly similar to the kind of view I have been describing: shifting the discussion from epistemological concerns to hermeneutical ones. I too recommend irony as a hermeneutical strategy to deal with life's "relativities." But the irony I propose is different from Rorty's in some important ways. First, I am interested in getting through modernity—or at least *seeing* through it—whereas Rorty's ironic project seems to say something like this: "The modern epistemological project fails because it is not possible to use human scientific reason to ground knowledge infallibly. The problem, however, is not with the values that brought us the modern epistemological paradigm but with our expectations and method of achieving the Enlightenment's goal of a worldview thoroughly grounded in human resources. The problem of modernity is not the emphasis on secular human rational resources but our optimism about grounding knowledge in them. This approach doesn't seem to work and produces some undesirable consequences, like intolerance and cruelty. Therefore we should continue to hope to achieve all of our goods as a human race through human effort and through something like human reason, only we should do so without basing it on *knowledge*."

Rorty, in other words, continues the modern secular project, he is just (slightly) more modest about human reason. He continues to think of the self in modern ways, as a self-sufficient entity that must actualize itself, and he continues the same pattern of modern thought inherited from Descartes, which thinks in terms of opposing dualities (Rorty's favorite oppositions are liberal/nonliberal and intellectual/nonintellectual). Because of this, Rorty is completely on the side of modernity when it comes to his basic picture of the world (read: myth of progress), and his strategy to save the sinking ship of modernity is to jettison the cargo. He thinks his ironic strategy will succeed by getting rid of values like truth and God, and so—to use Kierkegaardian terms—continues the modern fascination with genius.

My Kierkegaardian proposals of irony and edification are different. Edification is not directly related to a cultural project or something that done for us by the group. As I mean it, edification—or upbuilding (*opbyggene*), as Kierkegaard calls it—is about the formation of self, which certainly happens in and *through* social relations but is a task for each person to perform individually before God. In fact, some of Kierkegaard's harshest criticisms are reserved for those who defer this task to "the crowd" or "the herd" and simply capitulate to cultural forces to form and shape their selves. To be edified is to be built up as a self before God.

Furthermore, by my account, irony is a strategy that frees us from having to relate absolutely to truths that are quite obviously only relatively true. My ironist, like Rorty's, is someone who acknowledges the contingency of all our descriptions and our vocabularies and acknowledges that all our language and theories about reality ultimately do not have a (purely) objective leg to prop them up, that all our objective attempts to know reality and justify our beliefs about it are mere "approximations." I do not take this, however, as a thesis about *the possibility of truth* for humans but as a commentary on its *availability,* and in particular as a remark about *how* truth is available to us: truth cannot come to us (exclusively) in the form of objectively true statements that are grounded in or justified by human reason (alone). My ironist, therefore, acknowledges that objectively there are no vocabularies that have preferred justificatory status, but further recognizes that vocabularies may be preferable on some other basis—as is the case with revelation. As even Rorty will concede, a cultural process of edification is one reason we should prefer a particular vocabulary over another, and subsequently we should believe cruelty is the worst thing we can do.[49]

Kierkegaard never even tries to imagine edification without truth and sees irony as the form that edifying truth-telling takes during or after modernity. We can, of course, say objectively "true" things directly—like, for example, that it is −27°C outside this morning or that God was in Jesus Christ reconciling to himself the world. The point, however, is first that these sorts of objective "facts" or statements are only approximately true and are made from a finite, contingent perspective. And second, objective truths are only edifying

---

49. Rorty, *Contingency, Irony, and Solidarity*, xv; cf. 91–92. Here I am stringing together a line of thought that runs from Rorty's early emphasis on edification in *Philosophy and the Mirror of Nature* to his later emphasis on irony and solidarity in *Contingency, Irony, and Solidarity*.

when appropriately ironized and connected to our deeper values, interests, and concerns about being a good person (or living well). That
is, these objective truths (qua objective) are not ultimate, absolute,
or the exclusive form truth must eventually take for us to *be in* the
truth. The emphasis for Kierkegaard is always on irony as a strategy
to free up an individual to appropriate truth claims by pointing out
that the individual is treating something relative or "approximate" as
if it were absolute and necessary to believe. If my beliefs are necessary
or inevitable, I will have difficulty taking responsibility for believing
them. The goal of this ironizing process is that individuals are built
up or edified as they come to understand truths in connection with
their interests and goals and take responsibility for believing them.

It is this aspect of irony that makes it an important first step toward
an ethics of belief as well as the first moment of a postmodern and
hermeneutical view of truth. The need for irony arises out of the gap,
or wound, of reason alluded to in chapter 2. Truth-telling becomes
difficult in (post)modernity precisely because we lose our naive access
to truth and realize that absolute truth exists only for God. What
irony does for us in this situation is free us up to reappropriate the
content of belief. It makes possible an existential commitment to belief because the contingency of our situation is openly acknowledged
and our need to have ultimate or absolute answers is relativized. On
the one hand, this ironic stance challenges all of our attempts and
strategies to ground truth absolutely in human reason and make it our
possession. And yet, on the other hand, an ironic stance also ironizes
itself. It understands the basic distinction between a capital-T "Truth"
that stands for absolute Truth and a lowercase "truth" that stands
for contingent truths.[50] Because of this, the ironist realizes that our
inability to ground Truth absolutely does not rule out the possibility
of contingent truths that are adequate to our human situation. What
the ironist rejects, really, is something we may call "the deification of
the established order"[51]—the contingent, socially constructed perspec-

50. Merold Westphal makes the distinction between a first-order concept of Truth
(with a capital *T*) and a second-order concept of truth(s) in *Overcoming Onto-Theology* (New York: Fordham University Press, 2001), 95. I say more about truth in chap. 4.
51. Kierkegaard (Anti-Climacus) states in *Practice in Christianity*, ed. and trans.
Howard V. Hong and Edna H. Hong (Princeton: Princeton University Press, 1991), 91,

tive from which our community justifies its beliefs and practices. This kind of ironist grasps the Christian point that our failure to *be* the ground of Truth ourselves does not mean that we thereby avoid the responsibility to be in Truth's possession. While there is no guarantee that irony produces edification, it contributes to an ethics of belief precisely because it creates space for edification.[52]

The most important aspect of prophetic irony for my purposes here is that it creates the possibility of witnesses to the truth that can embody the Word they announce. A witness is someone who has encountered the truth, has been possessed by it, and then attempts to pass that truth along to someone else.[53] But the actual witnesses—the actual people, their lives—display or *show* the truth of what they announce and not just their words. The basis on which witnesses recommend to me the truth they have encountered, and by which they have been grasped, is that I too may be possessed by this truth and live in it.

Witness as Confession

Here it may be helpful to invoke Paul Ricoeur's discussion of the relationship between "testimony as narrative" and "testimony as act" to explain how witness works. Testimony, according to Ricoeur, has a "dialogic structure" in which there is a dynamic and mutually reinforcing tension between how I characterize the world (or what I claim is true about the world) and how I live in it.[54] I testify to what I have seen (or perceived) both by means of a verbal account or *story* relating how

---

that the "the deification of the established order is the secularization of everything." Mark Dooley links this to irony in *The Politics of Exodus: Kierkegaard and the Ethics of Responsibility* (New York: Fordham University Press, 2001), 55.

52. This also makes irony an important strategy to counteract ideology, which elevates the group over individuals and the rational over edification.

53. Kierkegaard states that a witness to the truth is "someone who proclaims the teaching and existentially expresses it." *Søren Kierkegaard's Journals and Papers*, vol. 6, ed. and trans. Howard V. Hong and Edna H. Hong, assisted by Gregor Malantschuk (Bloomington, IN: Indiana University Press, 1978), §6251.

54. Paul Ricoeur, "Emmanuel Levinas: Thinker of Testimony," in *Figuring the Sacred: Religion, Narrative, and Imagination*, trans. David Pellauer, ed. Mark I. Wallace (Minneapolis: Fortress, 1995), 108–26. I first discovered this reference in Rasmussen, *Between Irony and Witness*, 154–55.

I experienced a truth[55] and by how I *embody* that particular truth in my actions. Using this distinction as a general account, then, we can say that, as a Christian witness, I give narrative testimony to the word (or truth) I have received by telling my story of that encounter—how it has been received and how it has affected me or transformed me—so that I may help others better embody, and may myself better embody, that testimony in an earnest and passionate life that is concerned with being in the truth.[56] Whether the truth I proclaim is *true for me* will be evident from how I live—if that truth is appropriated by me as an integral part of how I live and act. This means the act of witness is much more like a *confession* of personal conviction than a logical argument for the objective truth of its propositions. Thus, from a prophetic standpoint, testimony as act *and* testimony as narration are critical parts of an edifying Christian witness. And the apologetic force of witnessing lies in the passionate integration of the message with the life of the witness. As a witness, I proclaim the truth not only with my lips but by my life. With my words I engage my listeners with a narrative so that they can imagine a world with this particular truth, and by my life I show them it is possible to live in that world.

As I just suggested, the act of confession is crucial to the concept of witness I am trying to develop. This dimension of witness is what distinguishes my postmodern paradigm from certain attempts to contrive an apologetic theology as a form of postmodern hermeneutics. Paul Lakeland articulates his postmodern apologetic theology in terms of Gadamer's "fusion of horizons." The theologian's task, Lakeland believes, is to "interpret society" from a rational perspective that maintains a kind of happy medium, not favoring wisdom from either the secular or sacred communities:

> In the fundamental, hermeneutical, apologetic moment in theology, the fusion of horizons occurs within the consciousness of the theologians and religious thinkers. The world questions the text (or

55. The wording here is important. For Ricoeur, testimony has what Vanhoozer describes as "a quasi-empirical meaning: though it is not the perception itself, it is the narration of a perception." Kevin J. Vanhoozer, *Biblical Narrative in the Philosophy of Paul Ricoeur* (Cambridge: Cambridge University Press, 1990), 259.

56. Cf. Rasmussen, *Between Irony and Witness*, 155.

narrative), and the text responds, adding its question in turn. This kind of theologian—in whom text and world meet—must speak the language of the tradition and the language of the world in which that tradition is to be represented. Neither language is to be preferred to the other.[57]

There is much with which to agree in this perspective. For one, I can think of no better description of a prophetic witness than Lakeland's description here of someone "in whom text and world meet." This is precisely how I understand the biblical depiction of prophets and apostles. And that is what places them squarely in the type of hermeneutical framework I described earlier. They are those who can narrate God's Word so powerfully that it engages the world's imagination. And they can do this just because they simultaneously speak the language of their tradition and are fluent in the language of the world. However, for biblical prophets the fusion of the horizon of their culture and the horizon of the Word they received occurs in their very *lives*, not only their consciousness. Prophetic speech stands at the intersection of the self and the crowd, the individual and the public, and calls persons—*these* people—to hear and encounter God in his Word. And this intersection occurs in *the very person* of the witness.

It is this public performance of witness that qualifies it as *confession*. The prophets and apostles *confess* their faith—they declare before the world, "This is what I believe. This is the truth I have encountered that has edified me. Take a look at my life, who I am, and see if you think that it's true. And I believe that if you consider your own life and appropriate this truth, you will find it is edifying for you too." Prophetic witness is a public act performed in the interests of edifying the community, and yet is a personal, private act as well. The appeal is not to universal norms of belief or to privileged insight into the nature of the "really real" or even to a contingent, provisional compromise that will enable differing points of view to coexist peacefully, but to a truth that may be edifying for everyone who embraces it. Thus, in the witness—the *person* who confesses—private

57. Paul Lakeland, *Postmodernity: Christian Identity in a Fragmented Age* (Mⁱ neapolis: Fortress, 1997), 88.

responsibility is embraced by public accountability so that the public and private spheres of life are united.[58]

But unlike Lakeland's public theologian, prophets and apostles quite clearly prefer the Word of the Lord to that of the crowd, and they are far more focused on calling people to encounter their God than on discovering the grammar for a universal experience of a higher power. They have no other gods than the Lord God and are not concerned with fusing his Word to the horizon(s) of human understanding so that they may produce a neutral and objectively true account of society or anything else. That would be, to invoke the Kierkegaardian distinction again, a case of privileging the genius over the apostle. Hence, the apologetic theology of Lakeland is also not postmodern in the way I am using the word. To think in terms of subsuming theological discourse in the horizon of human understanding is still to function within the modern apologetic paradigm. It displays a marked lack of irony about human reason and its potential. This so-called postmodern theology is simply a version of the modern liberal project rejiggered to accommodate certain critiques of the modern paradigm.

So instead of talking about "interpreting society," as Lakeland wishes to do, I would rather describe the apologist's job as that of interpreting society back to itself *theologically* in such a way that both the difference between *the way of the world* and *the Christian way of the cross* is made clear to it. It is a matter of "becoming locally explicit about Jesus," as John Howard Yoder has said, which involves "the particular experience of confessing Jesus here and now."[59] This is the heart of prophetic speech inasmuch as it is a call (back) to relationship with God and an enunciation of God's Word to us. The Word of God is always, Barth would say, an affront to all our human strategies to create meaning and significance apart from God, and all God's words to us call us from our self-sufficiency into a

58. Cf. David J. Gouwens, *Kierkegaard as Religious Thinker* (Cambridge: Cambridge University Press, 1996), 219.

59. John Howard Yoder, "The Disavowal of Constantine: An Alternative Perspective on Interfaith Dialogue," in *The Royal Priesthood: Essays Ecclesiological and Ecumenical* (Grand Rapids: Eerdmans, 1994), 253–54. Doug Harink provides a powerful explanation and application of Yoder in *Paul Among the Postliberals: Pauline Theology beyond Christendom and Modernity* (Grand Rapids: Baker Academic, 2003), 247–48.

relationship with God—and the Word God has spoken to us and to which we witness as Christians is Jesus Christ, who has shown us a much more excellent way.

Conclusion

The story of John recounted at the beginning of this chapter illustrates the phenomenon I previously described as the fragility of faith in our present secular age. Faith for us today is easy neither to obtain nor to maintain. For worse or better, there has been what Taylor describes as a "breach of naïveté" as modernity has changed the intellectual and existential contexts in which we do our believing. I also used John's encounter with the amateur apologists to demonstrate the unedifying nature of modern apologetics. John's issues with unbelief are not a straightforward matter of his being irrational or unaware of the issues involved in believing in God, and a rational apologetic argument is not going to show him the truth of Christian belief.

I have been mostly concerned in this chapter with describing how the objective and rational character of the discourse of modern apologetics is not edifying and does not qualify it as a spiritual curative for our (post)modern times. Instead of an *epistemology* of belief, I would like to propose an *ethics* of belief that is fundamentally hermeneutical in its approach. I wish to replace the professionalization of belief that inevitably occurs in modernity, where the only people qualified to witness, really, are the experts or "geniuses" who are brilliant enough to figure out clever apologetic arguments and strategies that show the epistemic superiority of Christian belief (or the Christian worldview). Instead, I suggest we change our metaphor or model of the apologist to that of the prophet or apostle who comes to us proclaiming a word they received from a personal encounter with God.

Prophetic speech is edifying because it is personal and ironic. It is focused on our personal relationship to the God who is and who speaks to us and calls us each into relationship with him. A witness that is prophetic in character is focused on *how* we believe rather than on the abstract, theoretical, and objective content of belief. The primary or driving concern is not to get people to agree or to acknowledge certain propositions or beliefs are true but rather that all persons—including the witness—be mutually edified in the truth. When edification is the goal and design, the moment of witness is a personal encounter and emerges from a relationship between persons. A witness is someone who has won a truth and then attempts to pass that truth along to another person. Through words, the witness narrates for listeners the categories that enable the witness to imagine the truth he or she wishes to show. This discourse is not directly under the control of the witness, nor is it grounded in rational abilities. Witness runs contrary to the established order of sense-making and creates the conceptual space for people to hear a word from God that challenges and subverts our staid and domestic processes for legitimizing beliefs. The word of witness speaks to another way of being in the world.

The full testimony of a witness, then, is the dialectic between what the witness professes and the manner in which this is embodied in the witness's life and actions. Taken together, these two elements are an ironic witness to the truth—of the sort we find put forward in Old Testament prophets like Ezekiel and Hosea. As Ezekiel acts out his prophecy in Ezekiel 4, it culminates with his baking a meal over a fire fueled with his own feces. And as part of his prophetic speech, Hosea marries a prostitute (or at least a habitually unfaithful woman), has children with her, and continues in faithfulness to her through all her infidelities. But, of course, the preeminent example of a witness to the truth who embodies the truth he proclaims is Jesus Christ—who *is* the message he brings. So the primary mark of a witness is that the witness is fully present in the message he or she carries. A witness's life expresses the message and embodies the truth the witness proclaims.

A witness of this sort has a much better chance of communicating the truth to someone like John, for whom faith is fragile and ephemeral. Coming to terms with the difficulty of faith requires a life lived faithfully before God. One possibility opened up by a hermeneutical approach is that a life of faith is more aptly articulated in terms of a struggle to be faith*ful*—to live truthfully—than as the possession of truths and absolute certainties. A faithful life is fidelity in, through, and despite the anxieties, uncertainties, and difficulties of belief in a secular age. Rather than thinking of the believer as the possessor of truth, who must then work ardently to maintain belief over against all rational challenges, it might be better to view the one who has faith as an "apprentice to truth."[60]

To speak of an apprentice to truth in this way is to acknowledge that truth is not our possession but something by which we must be possessed. I do not have the truth and cannot get it on my own. Instead, I must *apprentice*; I must submit myself to the tutelage of those who have mastered the requisite skills—or what the Greeks call *techne*, the knowledge that comes through exercising an *art*—in which I am not proficient. That is, I must engage in a different set of practices, learn a new vocabulary, be trained by "masters"—all of which presupposes that on my own I am not adequate to be in the truth. And this concept of apprenticing to the truth further recognizes that living in the truth is a *process* in which I learn how to be faithful. If I regard myself as an apprentice to the truth, I must be prepared to have my preconceptions and perceptions challenged, and I must be open to new avenues of understanding and interpreting my life through the texts and conceptual categories of faith as I learn how to be faithful in the ever-changing contexts of my life. As with any apprenticeship, there will be setbacks and failures as I learn how to be in truth's possession, and at times it may even appear I do not have much faith at all. The important thing will be that I maintain an essential interest in or fundamental concern with my life and its relation to truth (God), and that I never stop working this out in dialogue with the texts, practices, community, and relationships (i.e., the church) that present me with the concepts and categories to interpret my life in relation to God. This, to my mind, provides a way for us to think about faith in our (post)modern situation that can account for and witness to Christian truth, and cope with the fragile nature of faith in a secular age—at least much more so than any rational apologetic.

But prophetic speech has other characteristics that Christian apologists or witnesses would do well to attend to and that reorient apologetic witness more closely around the concept of edification. The traits I specifically have in mind are its *occasional* and *political*

---

60. David Wisdo uses this phrase in *The Life of Irony*, 135–38, but he borrows the term from Ralph Waldo Emerson. I mean something quite different by an apprentice to the truth than they do.

character and its being grounded in *love*. These set the agenda now for the final chapters of the book.

In the next chapter I return to the question of truth and try to be clearer as to what I mean when I link Christian truth to subjectivity and describe it in terms of edification. This leads us naturally into a discussion of the *eschatological* and *occasional* characteristics of Christian witness.

4

Witness and Truth

Christ is the truth in the sense that to *be* the truth is the
only true explanation of what truth is.[1]

Anti-Climacus

If you follow Jesus and don't end up dead, it appears you
have some explaining to do.[2]

Terry Eagleton

I have already talked about truth quite a lot. What I have said so far is
that approaching truth *epistemologically* in the modern sense—that
is, objectively, as something reflected in propositions (or statements),
then proven or justified logically and empirically—can be problematic
from a Christian standpoint for at least two reasons. First, we will be
continually frustrated in our attempts if we pursue truth objectively.
Contingent "approximations" are all we finite, fallible creatures have

1. Søren Kierkegaard, *Practice in Christianity*, ed. and trans. Howard V. Hong and
Edna H. Hong (Princeton: Princeton University Press, 1991), 205.
2. Terry Eagleton, *Faith, Reason, and Revolution: Reflections on the God Debate*
(New Haven: Yale University Press, 2009), 27.

available to us. Absolute, timeless Truth is God's alone. We perceive things from our various perspectives, within time, with these limited and changing bodies, and from the social contexts we inhabit. We won't, in other words, get to the bottom of reality to perceive reality as it *really* is apart from how it is *for us*. Second, pursuing truth exclusively in an objective way can also be problematic because it stymies our interests as persons or subjects. It limits our ability to *be* in the Truth. Propositions or statements considered in isolation from the persons who hold them and *how* they are held are meaningless and irrelevant to us. The more I seek to objectify the world and myself, the more I lose my *self*. And what does it profit a person if they gain the maximal set of justified, true beliefs but lose their own self?

I now wish to redescribe truth by changing metaphors from "correspondence" to *edification*.[3] I do this in order to avoid the modern split between objective and subjective (as if they were separate spheres of reality), which privileges objectivity in truth and denigrates an emphasis on subjectivity as a relativistic denial of truth. By my account, truth (as subjectivity) is the sort of thing people need and desire because it is *edifying*. That is, what matters about truth is that it builds me up, is true *for me*, and is the kind of thing that connects to my deepest concerns as a self. This is a different kind of reduplication than an objective relation between words and things. The change from correspondence to edification means truth is reproduced *in me*. Truth is edifying when I am in its thrall, so to speak, when I am in *its* possession and I live in such a way that it explains me to myself and enables and empowers me to live honestly and meaningfully—with a clear *conscience*—with God and others.[4]

3. I am oversimplifying by using "correspondence" to stand for all objective and representational theories of truth. The point I am trying to make is that I wish to shift from metaphors that stand for an objective approach to truth to a metaphor that brings to the fore subjective concerns about truth.

4. I am sensitive to the charge of conflating truth with justification when thinking about knowledge. That is to say, we must not think that the truth-value of a belief (whether it is objectively true or false) is dependent on our being able to show it to be true or at least that it is reasonable to believe (i.e., its justification). This is a complaint that is sometimes brought against those who have an "epistemic" view of truth, which says (roughly) that a statement is made true by how it connects to other beliefs a person has, by those who have a "realist" view of truth, which says (roughly) that statements are made true by factors outside the beliefs of any person. For a general discussion of

But none of this means that we cannot think and speak about truth in objective terms *at all*. Edification is not merely a private event. As Kevin Vanhoozer reminds us, "one stands for truth because truth stands for everyone."[5] When we speak about edification and witness, we are never talking about a purely private relation to anything, however much we are referring to the actions and states—the edification—of an individual person. There is something of an intrapersonal and public element to truth, and because we are social beings, the edification of an individual person necessarily takes place within a community of other persons who share (very nearly) the same commitments, values, and vocabularies. One might say that the hiddenness of edification is recognizable by its fruits.[6]

This being the case, when I witness to a truth that edifies me, I recommend it to someone else as potentially true or edifying for them as well. Here the paradigm of truthful speech might well be, as Vanhoozer suggests, Martin Luther's famous (if somewhat historically dubious) declaration before the Diet of Worms: "Here I stand. I can do no other."[7] In the elegant formula "Here I stand" we see that the private individual, Martin Luther, displays a passion to see truth made public. He desires for everyone to be edified by the truth that is true for him. Luther does not pretend to offer the absolute Truth; he confesses a truth that is thoroughly conditioned by his perspective and context. He stands *here*, right *now*, attesting to *this truth*, and he can do no other because his *conscience* forbids it. But his stand signifies his conviction and commitment that the truth by which he is edified is true for everyone.

this, see Bruce D. Marshall, *Trinity and Truth* (Cambridge: Cambridge University Press, 2000), 223–24. I do not believe my attempt to describe truth in terms of edification is susceptible to this charge, because (1) edification is not an epistemic entity—it actually is a form of realism about truth; and (2) like other forms of correspondence, my formal claim is that *being edified* is itself the truth-relation; establishing that one has been edified or drawing out criteria for edification is a completely different issue, one that I address below. I have almost no interest, however, in spelling this out analytically.

5. Kevin J. Vanhoozer, *First Theology: God, Scripture and Hermeneutics* (Downers Grove, IL: InterVarsity, 2002), 366–67.

6. Cf. Kierkegaard's chapter "Love's Hidden Life and Its Recognizability by Its Fruits," in *Works of Love*, ed. and trans. Howard V. Hong and Edna H. Hong (Princeton: Princeton University Press, 1995), 5–16.

7. See Vanhoozer, *First Theology*, 366–67, for this and the following discussion.

So when I say truth is edifying and is approached through subjectivity, I do not mean it is private and personal in the sense that only I have access to it. The truth that edifies is never disconnected from its cognitive content. That is, truth is not edifying apart from what the statement or words used are trying to say (what some call its propositional content) and do. And truth ceases to be edifying for me when it is based on fantasy or stems from a narcissistic picture of myself.[8] But the cognitive content of truth taken apart from its subjective relation to my life (my interests, desires, passions—in short, all that makes me a person) are merely *adiaphora*, or things of indifference or irrelevance. Edifying truth, however, is in some meaningful way both public and objective, if by these terms we indicate that a truth depends on something outside of the edified person that contributes to truthfulness.

From the standpoint of Christian witness and apologetics, this raises important questions, first about the nature of Christian truth claims, and second whether they can be verified. I treat these in order.

Truth after Metaphysics

The modern concern with truth marks a sharp departure from the premodern focus on natural substances that make the world what it is and, in turn, make it possible for our words or thoughts about them to be true.[9] It is because things are already true to *themselves* that premoderns believe we can perceive, think, or talk about them truly. Prior to modernity, just as with reason and rationality, it is the *cosmos* and its being—the way it *is*—that make our thoughts and our words about it possible. It is because things have forms or essences that are identical to themselves, as it were, that our minds and our words can ever have any truth in them. This is not the case, however, for moderns who reject the old-world cosmology. Modern thinkers tend to believe that our thoughts and statements can be true

8. Cf. Eagleton, *Faith, Reason, and Revolution*, 122.
9. Barry Allen narrates this shift quite nicely (albeit with a completely different end in mind) in Barry Allen, *Truth in Philosophy* (Cambridge, MA: Harvard University Press, 1993), 9–40.

when the things we speak and think about are self-evidently the same as our words and thoughts. They skip over the middle term—the forms or essences of things—and jump straight to a comparison between words and things. The vehicle of the comparison is called a *proposition*—or whatever is expressed by a declarative sentence in a natural language.

So truth in modernity is *propositional*. Or at least it tends to be.[10] As we saw in chapter 1 with William Lane Craig's apologetic methodology, this means we tend to think of truth exclusively as a property of the words and declarative sentences we use to refer to things in the world, such as "It is snowing outside" and "The car is white." These sentences are *true* only if the things referred to actually are the same as what has been said. So "It is snowing outside" is true if in fact it is snowing outside.[11] What is especially handy about propositional truths is that they make perfect candidates for the kind of knowledge moderns are interested in. Sentences[12] are special kinds of objects that present us with information in an objective form, which means they can be objectively examined and justified and can be expressed in any context. And they have the added benefit of bringing clarity, because, at least on the face of it, declarative sentences are either true or false. Sentences express truths without degrees, so to speak; or we might say that they are absolute truths.[13] If it is snowing outside right now, then it is never true to say that it is *not* snowing outside right now. Propositional truths are also *neutral* in the sense that the truth of a

10. A propositional view of truth has certainly been the dominant view. Some, like J. P. Moreland ("Truth, Contemporary Philosophy, and the Postmodern Turn," *Journal of the Evangelical Theological Society* 48 [2005]: 84), may try to avoid certain problems with propositions and think of truth as *conceptual*, so that what makes a thought true is that it presumably has an ontological correspondence to that which it is of. One trouble with a view such as this, of course, is that it still has the difficulty of explaining how the sentences we use to express our thoughts are true.

11. As indicated earlier, I am aware of the debate over epistemic and minimalist views of truth that argue against this way of understanding truth. They are not, however, the dominant tradition in Western thinking, especially Christian thinking.

12. I am being informal here. Technically, of course, a proposition is what is expressed by a sentence in a natural language. Many different sentences in a host of natural languages may express the same proposition.

13. Note that the sense in which I use the term "absolute truths" here is a matter of *degrees* and not *necessity*. "It is snowing outside" is never, in my opinion, a necessary truth, however completely true it may be.

sentence is not dependent on any qualities of the person who utters or believes it. If it is snowing outside, then "It is snowing outside" is always and absolutely true even if I am stark raving mad when I say it. These objective and neutral truths, in turn, are also those that are in principle open to public verification by any and every one. They are, in other words, universal. The truth about something tells us the way it really is, and does that in a way that no other description of it could also be true.

What I am trying to draw attention to is the fact that modern thinkers—including modern apologists who defend or attempt to show the objective, propositional truth of Christianity—have a profoundly *un*ironic approach to truth. They believe humans grasp the full and complete truth about things as they really are. There is a basic inability for moderns to make a distinction between first-order Truth (with a capital *T*) and second-order, contingent truths (with a lowercase *t*) that recognizes the irony of making assertions or holding beliefs from perspectives that are themselves revisable and not ultimate. Underneath the discussion of truth in modernity lies some version of what Barry Allen refers to as "truth's *ontological a priori*."[14] This means, roughly, that our thoughts, statements, and so on are true only if they re-present us with things as they *really* are. The modern approach to truth, in other words, is deeply *metaphysical*. It defines truth in such a way that our access to truth depends upon our ability to comprehend what is really real about the world and to say it or think it exactly that way. First-order Truth makes a critical assumption about the adequacy of the human mind to deliver the Truth about reality as it really is—the classical notion of *adequatio rei et intellectus* (the agreement/adequation of thing and intellect). We might say that when we think about it this way, Truth is represented by the knowledge of God—it gives us access to the way in which God views the world.[15]

For my part, I am deeply suspicious of this metaphysical approach to the truths that exist for us humans. One way of labeling my focus

14. Allen, *Truth in Philosophy*, 31–32. Although Allen does not define truth's ontological *a priori* in quite the same way I do, the idea is basically his.
15. Cf. Merold Westphal, *Overcoming Onto-Theology* (New York: Fordham University Press, 2001), 95.

on edification, then, is to see it as an attempt to talk about *post-metaphysical* truth. I am interested in how we think and speak about truth when we no longer think it possible to spell out exactly how our words and thoughts match up with reality, and when we believe our words and minds cannot do so exactly or exhaustively. What happens to truth, then? I do not believe we need to throw out the concept of truth simply because the modern concept is problematic and deeply troubling. My suggestion is that when we wish to talk about truth objectively, we do so in terms of truth spelled with a lowercase *t*—which represents the kind of finite, fallible knowledge available to us humans. This signals the best we can do from the limited perspectives we inhabit.

At this point, no doubt, many readers (if they are still reading) are nervous. It is tempting to think Christianity necessarily trades in absolute truths and, in that sense, a Christian witness must be committed to metaphysical truth. After all, one of the things Christians are witness to is that they have been gripped by a Higher Being who is the clue to the meaning of all that is. It is understandably difficult to see how a passion for Truth—God's Truth—or any witness who is gripped by the Truth can possibly avoid speaking and thinking in terms of metaphysical truth. Merold Westphal observes that "when we hear Augustine panting, 'Truth! Truth! How the very marrow of my soul within me yearned for it' ([*Confessions*] III:6), we might think him engaged in the 'metaphysical' project of rendering the whole of reality intelligible to human understanding."[16]

This temptation to think of witness in terms of metaphysical truth is partly forestalled, however, when we remember that I do not think the Christian witness actually *is* a prophet or apostle. There is a critical disanalogy we as Christian witnesses have to the prophets. We testify to the truths by which we have been edified as we "work out [our] own salvation with fear and trembling" (Phil. 2:12); *actual prophets* speak the words of God with God's authority. Augustine comes to a similar conclusion in book 12 of his *Confessions* as he wrestles with various interpretations of the biblical account of creation, trying to discern which is the Truth about the matter (that is, "what Moses

16. Ibid., 277.

had in mind when he wrote 'In the beginning God created the heaven and the earth'").[17]

We can learn some important lessons from St. Augustine about how to be a Christian witness and at the same time avoid a metaphysical approach to truth. In his *Confessions*, Augustine runs into a problem while trying to choose between the various Christian interpretations of the Genesis account of creation. His trouble is that the different interpretations of the Genesis creation account *all* seem to be true! He concludes that there really are a "diversity of true views" and confesses that he himself does not know which is *the Truth*.[18] Augustine settles instead for the conclusion "that these texts [of Scripture] contain various truths" and perspectives about one and the same matter and that we should be guided in our interpretations by what is edifying. God *himself* is the Truth and the "fount of truth" as well as the object of our passion for Truth. The contingent truths we affirm from Scripture, however, are those that engender "the reader's spiritual profit."[19]

According to Westphal, the striking thing about Augustine's account of truth in his *Confessions* is that Augustine remains ever-mindful of the personal, passional context for any human engagement with truth. Augustine himself feels and expresses this passion and never forgets that the appropriate focus of this passion is not on propositional truth but instead on "the *wisdom* of eternal truth."[20] Augustine therefore subordinates all propositional truth to God himself who is the eternal Truth, the personal Being who, as a person, is the ultimate object of our passion for truth and is the origin of

17. Saint Augustine, *Confessions*, trans. Henry Chadwick (Oxford: Oxford University Press, 1991), 264. I am indebted to The Reverend Joseph Walker for pointing out this section of Augustine's *Confessions* to me.

18. Ibid., 270.

19. Ibid. In this text, Augustine actually affirms a dual criterion for the contingent truths we affirm as those "which supremely [correspond] to the light of truth *and* to the reader's spiritual profit" (my emphasis). By "[corresponds] to the light of truth," I take Augustine to refer to something like the careful and rigorous application of our God-given (and God-governed) cognitive abilities to apprehend contingent truths through an engagement in the interpretive tradition of Christianity. I have emphasized the latter condition because it is germane to my argument here.

20. From Augustine's *Confessions* 3.4 and cited in Westphal, *Overcoming Onto-Theology*, 277 (my emphasis). Cf. Saint Augustine, *Confessions*, 39.

all wisdom and knowledge. This is a radically ironic move that puts Truth outside of our grasp and mastery.

For Augustine, then, *God* sets the agenda in our pursuit of truth, and God's agenda is love. Christian truth, Augustine believes, is not about finding the answers to all our questions, nor is it focused on discovering the objective principles of the universe so that we may gain some leverage or control over it and others. When God's person is the goal of our pursuit of truth, it is a personal encounter that has edification at its center. For Christians, Truth becomes virtually indistinguishable from Love, and being in the truth is synonymous with transcending ourselves in love for the other. "In the final analysis," Westphal explains, "knowledge is *aufgehoben* [nullified, fulfilled, or caught up] in its proper telos, love of God (of which praise is a part) and neighbor (both friend and enemy)."[21]

This introduces a theme that I develop more in chapter 5—namely, that Christian truth and witness is intimately connected to the command to love. For his part, Kierkegaard describes the believer as "a lover" who could not imagine trying to demonstrate the truth of her love by rational arguments and evidences, as if her love was establish by these things rather than a direct, personal relationship to her beloved.[22] Be that as it may, the significance of this account of Augustine's view of truth in his *Confessions* is that it describes a Christian passion for truth that avoids the trappings of metaphysical truth and the modern emphasis on propositions. Truth for Augustine is not *our* possession but *God's*—it is, in fact, God's person and not ever our words about God! And our passion for truth is to be *in* the Truth, not merely to know it objectively through propositions.

I want to make one further suggestion about truth before moving on. There remains something deep and mysterious about the truths we speak and think—at least at the level of theory. I want to propose that the best way to think about truth in terms of its objectivity is in terms of *language games* (or a similar concept). This, of course, is the terminology Wittgenstein uses in his later philosophy as he tries to

21. Westphal, *Overcoming Onto-Theology*, 277–78.
22. Søren Kierkegaard, *Sickness Unto Death*, ed. and trans. Howard V. Hong and Edna H. Hong (Princeton: Princeton University Press, 1980), 103–04. Terry Eagleton in *Faith, Reason, and Revolution*, 120, also comments on this passage in Kierkegaard.

work out a way of thinking about language that avoids the problems of modern philosophy.[23] The significance of this is that it connects language and our truth-telling to the meaningful activities in which we engage with others. In Wittgenstein's sense, I understand language games as more than just rules for speaking.[24] They are embedded in the ways we act together when we perform specific tasks or social practices, like bricklaying, painting, or praying. These practices are "rule-governed" in that they include implicit rules for how to act and speak correctly within that practice. Good masons know the "rules" for good bricklaying, as well as how to speak truly about it. The same is true of painting, praying, and so on. This means the languages we speak and the truths we tell, and even the insights we have, are all set within the contexts of the social and cultural practices of our various and sundry communities, which form *perspectives* through which we perceive the world and apprehend truths. But it also means that when we try to theorize about truth (that is, when we try to describe what truth *is*) using concepts like "correspondence"—so that we can somehow get at it from behind, underneath, or outside the concrete practices in which we make, speak, and act—we will not have much luck. There is no further illumination to be had in that direction. We keep hitting dead ends. The concept of truth, at bottom, resists deeper analysis. So there is a kind of theoretical ambiguity about truth that ultimately we will have to content ourselves with, quite apart from the very definite, practical certainty of truth we gain from participating in various practices. The concept of truth is, as Donald Davidson has argued, one of the most fundamental and obvious concepts we have, and therefore it stubbornly resists enlightenment by other, less clear concepts (like "correspondence") we may use to explain it.[25]

Objectively speaking, though, the truths to which we witness enjoy what we might call a *potential* universality. They do not have

23. Ludwig Wittgenstein, *Philosophical Investigations*, 2nd ed., trans. G. E. M. Anscombe (London: Basil Blackwell, 1967).

24. See Fergus Kerr, *Theology after Wittgenstein*, 2nd ed. (London: Society for Promoting Christian Knowledge, 1997) for an exceptionally clear and helpful account of Wittgenstein's philosophy and its relevance to Christian theology.

25. Donald Davidson, "The Folly of Trying to Define Truth," in *Truth*, ed. Simon Blackburn and Keith Simmons (Oxford: Oxford University Press, 1999), 308–9.

metaphysical essences that are rationally available to all rational be-ings, and yet whenever I think or express myself in language, my thoughts or words are incipiently universal insofar as they *may* be understood by others. The categories and rules of language are inher-ently public, not private, shared at very least by others who inhabit the same language games and engage in the practices and behaviors I do. Since we humans inhabit the world under fundamentally simi-lar conditions, with similar bodies, needs, desires, and practices, we possess the potential to understand each other. But a description of how and why this is possible does not need to appeal to universal essences or any other aspect of a metaphysical account of truth to be made intelligible.

For example, Maurice Merleau-Ponty adopts the language of "lat-eral universals" or "transversals" in order to convey the universalizing possibilities for meaning and human languages. Instead of metaphysi-cal essences, what makes our speech (and our truths) imaginable by others are lateral universals that occur through the overlapping of one person's experience with that of others. But, at the same time, these lateral universals maintain the uniqueness and specificity of each person's experience. Merleau-Ponty explains:

> If universality is attained, it will not be through a universal language which would go back prior to the diversity of languages to provide us with the foundations of all possible languages. It will be through an oblique passage from a given language that I speak and that initiates me into the phenomenon of expression, to another given language that I learn to speak and that effects the act of expression according to a completely different style—the two languages (and ultimately all given languages) being contingently comparable only at the outcome of this passage and only as signifying wholes, without our being able to recognize in them the common elements of one single categorical structure.[26]

Notice, first, that the universality of language is something that may be *attained* and is not something inherent or given. The type of

26. Maurice Merleau-Ponty, *Signs*, trans. Richard McCleary (Evanston, IL: North-western University Press, 1964), 87.

universality spoken of here is not one that is necessary or inevitable, and neither is it a transcendent principle that grounds different identities and provides a basis for comparison of sameness and difference. Here we have a view of human languages that is consistent with the basic elements I just described—human languages are language *games* in the sense that they are not derived from a single, rational foundation but from our practices. We are not trapped in our language games, but the languages we speak—their terms of reference, their truths, their sense, and so on—are always potentially understandable by those outside of them (although, not necessarily straightaway and definitely not by the sheer force of our rational capabilities). To understand me, someone will have to spend time mastering the language game I speak, as well as carefully attending to my life. And their ability to understand me will depend on the degree to which they accomplish these actions.

It is important to underscore that in my description here, language and culture create the *possibility* for our (finite, fallible, and contingent) experience of truth rather than act as a *barrier* to truth. This is just as true for the Christian gospel and the truths we use to express it as it is for bricklaying. The gospel truths we proclaim as witnesses are, in a manner of speaking, the gospel-as-we-have-encountered-it within the community and practices of those who confess Jesus as their Lord. And the specific truths we witness reflect how we have understood the gospel from within our particular cultural moment. It does not follow from this, however, that these truths are therefore *false* or *relative* in any absolute and final way.

Westphal explains that perspectivism of this sort is relative *only* in the sense that it makes

> the dual claim that our insights, whether they be factual or normative, are relative to the standpoint from which they are made, and that the standpoint we occupy (even when making this claim) inevitably betrays that it is not an absolute standpoint, an all-inclusive, "totalizing" point of view that sees everything and is blind to nothing.[27]

27. Merold Westphal, "Of Stories and Languages," in *Christianity and the Postmodern Turn*, ed. Myron B. Penner (Grand Rapids: Brazos, 2005), 152. I am indebted to Westphal for the Pauline reference in this section as well.

In short, this perspectivism is relative only in that it insists our thoughts are not God's and only God is absolute. St. Paul speaks of this kind of perspectivism when he attests "for now we see in a mirror, dimly" and "we know only in part, and we prophesy only in part" (1 Cor. 13:12, 9). This may (and I insist that it does in fact) mean that we must maintain a more modest claim as to the absoluteness of our particular theological systems, but it does not mean we surrender the truth of the gospel altogether—in fact, this gospel truth depends on and is relative to the absolute Truth of the gospel revealed to us in Jesus.

I should make one final point about my "postmetaphysical" concept of truth. I do not deny there is a real world that exists independently of human minds or suggest we never encounter reality. I do not think, for example, that all we ever experience are our own thoughts. My emphasis on perspectivism and the subjectivity of truth is entirely compatible with a firm conviction that there is an external world and that, as G. K. Chesterton once said, reality is precisely what we bump into while we are thinking of something else. While I try to avoid insisting that reality must be a certain way, it is important to recognize this reluctance to describe how things really are is more a species of metaphysical *agnosticism*, which remains undecided about how to characterize (theoretically) the exact nature of reality, than that of metaphysical *atheism*, which actively denies the existence of an external reality. Whenever we speak, we imply a certain picture of the world—or, better, a story that tells us what the world might be like in its broad features. This does not mean, however, that whenever I speak, I imply that I may describe what the world is really like in terms of its metaphysical essences.

So that is the status of our language and thoughts about God or any other theological desiderata. If a question is asked about the nature of Christian truth claims—for example, creeds and doctrines—my answer is they are fallible, human expressions (interpretations) of the truths Christians have won for themselves in their various contexts. They are, in other words, the best rendering a Christian community could give, given their concerns and interests within the specific contexts and Christian practices in which they formulated the truth claims. They are normative—for we Christians, who share similar interests and concerns as part of the same church, continue to find them edifying as part of our own confession of Jesus as Lord within our various cultures and practices.

This point needs to be understood carefully in light of my earlier insistence on viewing Christian belief as occurring within a hermeneutical tradition—a set of texts that are part of the ongoing conversation of a diverse and ever-widening community of people.[28] If we take this view, we will understand ourselves *and* our edification as significantly related to the confessions of our fellow believers. One may always question us as to why our edification is specifically *Christian* edification, and this will have to be answered (at least partly) in reference to something like the Christian tradition—or, better, the church.[29] As I have said already, edification is not merely a private event that I can interpret for myself and all by myself. It is entirely possible—indeed, we should expect—that others may have more insight into my edification than I do. And I may not feel particularly edified when really I am. So we cannot naively (and arrogantly) dispense with the truths that have been confessed and witnessed to by our forbearers or those in other

28. John R. Franke reminds us that the Christian tradition is not "a religion of cultural uniformity," as Lamin Sanneh has put it, and cannot be captured in a single perspective, so that "the ongoing confession and proclamation of the church, understood corporately, constitutes the diverse and manifold witness of the church to the truth of the gospel of Jesus Christ in its various and historical embodiments." *Manifold Witness: The Plurality of Truth* (Nashville: Abingdon, 2009), 37.

29. Some may be tempted to object that there is no such thing as *the* Christian tradition—just a ragtag collection of beliefs and practices stretched out over cultures, times, and geography—and that any attempt to identify a Christian tradition is completely forced and artificial. While it is true that as a living tradition Christianity has incredible diversity in both belief and practice, I find this line of thinking unhelpful. It adopts a rather narrow approach to defining Christianity, which says that there can only be *one* right way to believe in and follow Jesus, and that we must be able to draw the circle so that *all* fit in it—and then argues that if this attempt at definition fails, there is no such thing as the Christian tradition. I prefer instead to think in terms of a confessional center (of belief and practice) that loosely defines the Christian tradition, rather than a circumference. We may then approximate where different things stand relative to that center. There will be some fuzziness the further we go from the center, but some things clearly are in close relation to it, while others are, for all intents and purposes, not much in relation to the center at all. John Franke's *Manifold Witness* is very helpful in showing how the cultural diversity of Christian confession is a gift, not a curse, to the church and is part of its witness to the triune God of Christian faith who is "a plurality-in-unity and a unity-in-plurality" (17).

cultures and places. They stand as a sign to us, a challenge even, of the edification that can be ours if our lives are shaped significantly by the same confessions and practices. This is not a naive or blind acceptance of tradition or the dictates of one's community, because truth is not something that is ever under human control. From a Christian standpoint, the very notion of truth stands for the affirmation that in relation to God we are always in the wrong and that being in the truth is our project.[30] It requires faith—a second naïveté.

Thus, a very important dialectic is opened up between the individual and his or her tradition, whereby the individual is guided by tradition but *in another sense* also stands over against tradition as someone who must own it personally. As one who understands the shortcomings and contingencies of every human rational effort—including the Christian tradition—I must come to see for myself how the faith I received is *true for me*. In short, I must come to see I am edified by it. This standing over against tradition is not a judgment on it as such. In fact, it signifies an ongoing and deep commitment to the authority of tradition, as well as a passionate belief in the goals and practices of tradition. (As St. Peter declares in John's Gospel, "Lord, to whom can we go? You have the words of eternal life," John 6:68.) As an individual believer I do not sit in authority over Scripture or tradition, but I must wrestle with them and struggle to make them mine and resituate their truths within my time, my life, and my community, through Christian practices I appropriate as my own.

Christian Truth-Telling

I have addressed the first of my opening questions about truth, describing what I think the general character of Christian truth claims to be. To say it in a sentence, they are second-order, contingent, perspectival truths that do not give us God's perspective on himself, but nevertheless are normative for us. In turning to our second question

30. This is taken from the title of the sermon appended to Søren Kierkegaard, *Either/Or*, part 2, ed. and trans. Howard V. Hong and Edna H. Hong (Princeton: Princeton University Press, 1987), "The Upbuilding That Lies in the Thought That in Relation to God We Are Always in the Wrong," whose last line states that "only the truth that builds you up is truth for you" (354).

about how Christian truths are verified, I find the issue is inextricably bound up with the nature of Christian truth-telling. The proof of Christian witness is always in the pudding. The pudding in this case is our *lives* as witnesses—our overall patterns of action and behavior (including our thoughts, feelings, and dispositions). If we return to Luther's confession "Here I stand" and take it as a paradigmatic act of Christian witness and truth-telling,[31] we see that Luther's conviction—the fruits of his being edified—is made clear by *what* he does and *how* he does it.

We can look at Luther's testimony as an instance of what Paul Ricoeur calls *attestation*. Ricoeur prefers to use the concept of attestation to identify the kind of truth-procedure or certainty that accompanies testimony, in contrast to the kind of certainty involved in making epistemological truth claims.[32] Witnesses *attest* to their truths. Attestation is a form of belief, to be sure, but Ricoeur explains that it is not an abstract, epistemological "belief *that*"; it is, rather, a more subjective "belief *in*," which nevertheless is in no way inferior to knowledge. To attest to something is really a form of trust. When I attest to something, I implicitly invoke "a trust in the power to say, in the power to do, in the power to recognize [my]self as a character in a narrative, in the power, finally, to respond to accusation."[33] Ricoeur, in fact, expressly links attestation to *conscience*—the very basis on which Luther makes his appeal. "Conscience," Ricoeur writes, "is, in truth, that place par excellence in which illusions about oneself are intimately bound up with attestation."[34] What we find here is that, for Ricoeur, attestation is an ironic form of truth-telling that happens always in the first person. I am always present in my attestations, making them as myself and in my own name, but never under the illusion that I am

31. Principally, *the* paradigmatic act of truth-telling is Jesus's incarnation (from birth through life, death, and resurrection), so beautifully described by St. Paul in his letter to the Philippians: "who, though he was in the form of God, did not regard equality with God as something to be exploited, but emptied himself . . . humbled himself and became obedient to the point of death. . . . Therefore God also highly exalted him" (Phil. 2:6–9).

32. Paul Ricoeur, *Oneself as Another*, trans. Kathleen Blamey (Chicago: University of Chicago Press, 1992), 21.

33. Ibid., 22.

34. Ibid., 341.

objectively justified in what I attest or that it is infallibly true. That is to say, conscience contains an imperative to interact with others, to attest to ourselves in the presence of another.[35]

I introduce the concept of attestation for two reasons. The first is to outline how it might be possible to witness to truth without claiming epistemic certainty about it. Objectively, attestation is risky. I place myself on the line and do not (necessarily) enjoy the luxury of rational justification for my assertions. When I attest to something, I believe *in* what I assert and connect myself to the assertion with a kind of certainty we might describe as subjective. This is to counteract the antidogmatic stance we often find today in modern theology, which displays what Slavoj Žižek calls a kind of "suspended belief" that survives only as "an obscene secret" that is never fully admitted publically.[36] Some Christians appear to think that we should modestly accept that all positions are relative, conditioned by contingent historical factors, so that no one has any definitive purchase on the truth. For them the task of theology is to render our Christian religious experience intelligible in terms that any intelligent, reasonable, and responsible person (with a refined set of Western liberal democratic values) can understand and evaluate according to "accepted" public criteria. "Christianity is just the way *I* worship God," they might say. "You, no doubt, worship him under a different name. You have your truth and I have mine."[37] When one adopts an attitude like this, it is not difficult to see how attesting to Christian truths will not seem a necessary part of faith.

35. Ricoeur writes, "Conscience appears as the inner assurance that, in some particular circumstance, sweeps away doubt, hesitation, the suspicion of inauthenticity, hypocrisy, self-compliance, and self-deception, and authorizes the acting and suffering human being to say: here I am." Paul Ricoeur, "From Metaphysics to Moral Philosophy," *Philosophy Today* (Winter 1996), 454.

36. Slavoj Žižek, "Rhetorics of Power," *Diacritics* 31, no. 1 (Spring 2001), 103. I should clarify that for Žižek, who follows Jacques Lacan's psychoanalytic thought closely, something is "obscene" when it is publically disavowed but secretly (privately or un-/subconsciously) acknowledged as a necessary supplement to what is avowed—even though it contradicts what is avowed. One of Žižek's favorite examples of this is political liberalism, which is publically against violence, but "secretly" depends upon it to sustain its way of life.

37. This is the theological legacy of someone like John Hick, *God Has Many Names* (Philadelphia: Westminster Press, 1982). Although the position I stated is a caricature of someone as philosophically sophisticated as Hick, I often encounter this exact caricature in those who adopt his general position but are less nuanced than he is.

This attitude appears to be either a continued hankering after metaphysical truth (only as a kind of despair about achieving it) or something like a failure to have a genuine faith at all. In effect it claims that "the Truth is that there is no Truth, and therefore every truth is equally in/valid." Placed alongside my account of subjectivity and truth, this sort of modern, liberal-minded, pluralistic relativism suggests, at best, that such a Christian is only at the beginning stages of edification and that the individual's life and perspective have not been sufficiently shaped by the truths of faith to attest to them. At worst, it might imply that such a Christian has not been edified by Christian truths at all—that such truths are mere intellectual curiosities. Somewhere in between the two extremes may be Christians who actually are edified by their faith but remain so caught in their circumstance (i.e., the modern paradigm) that they continually second-guess their consciences and therefore lack the full confidence required for attestation. Whatever the case, if we really are not concerned about achieving the (absolute) Truth as God sees it, if we really do not believe that achieving the Truth is necessary to attaining normative Christian truths, and if we further configure our thinking about Christian truth around edification, then it seems to me that we will have the ability to attest to the contingent, fallible truths that edify us.[38] In our Christian witness we always testify—as Luther does—from our conscience and not from an epistemically secure and objectively demonstrable position. The Christian witness says: "Here I stand. I cannot do anything else. I cannot refuse to acknowledge this truth, because it is the one that is true for me and has shaped me into the self I am."

38. Žižek lets loose with an entertaining rant against the use of "undecidability" as the basis for a less than full, existential commitment to one's beliefs: "Is the same falsity not clearly discernible in the rhetoric of many a postmodern deconstructionist? Is their apparently modest relativization of their own position not the mode of appearance of its very opposite, of privileging their own position of enunciation, so that one can effectively claim that the self-relativizing stance is a key ingredient in today's rhetorics of power? Compare the struggle and pain of the 'fundamentalist' with the serene peace of the liberal democrat who, from a safe subjective position, ironically dismisses every fully pledged engagement, every 'dogmatic' taking sides. Consequently, yes, I plead guilty: in this choice, I without hesitation opt for the 'fundamentalist.'" Žižek, "Rhetorics of Power," 103.

The second reason I introduce Ricoeur's concept of attestation is to show that when we view truth as edification, truth-telling is *agonistic*. It is a struggle (*agon* = "struggle" or "contest"). Truth-telling is a process of attesting to the truth of our convictions. It is not a snap shot of reality but more like a dramatic portrayal of how things may be when the rule and reign of Christ is expressed in and through our lives.[39] Christian truth is an *aleitheia*—an uncovering, disclosing, or making visible the very presence of God among us.[40] And this uncovering is concrete and actual, not abstract and intellectual. Christian truth-telling, therefore, is a field of performance and an acting or living out of the truth that is edifying and upbuilding. This is not merely an objective apprehension or formal acknowledgment—we must win these truths for ourselves and make them our own. It is not an instant calculation that is over and then done with, but the undertaking of a lifetime. As I have mentioned several times already, the truth to which Christians witness is not the sort of truth that one *has*, but the sort of truth that one *is*.

Thus, truth for the Christian is a *task*, and the task is not to *know* the truth intellectually but to *become* the truth. For this reason Kierkegaard connects belief, truth, and suffering. Belief shapes us into who we are, and the truth—the kind that edifies us—rubs off the rough corners and molds us into the kind of selves that can both attest to them and express them with our lives.[41] Christian witness, then, also

39. This performative dimension in my account of witness may be what distinguishes it from the very helpful proposals for postmodern witness of both Richard Bauckham in *Bible and Mission: Christian Witness in a Postmodern World* (Grand Rapids: Baker Academic, 2003) and James K. A. Smith in *Who's Afraid of Postmodernism? Taking Derrida, Lyotard, and Foucault to Church* (Grand Rapids: Baker Academic, 2006), whose emphases appear to be more on the cognitive and foundational importance of the verbal proclamation of the biblical story. I should also note that Kevin Vanhoozer makes use of the metaphor of drama to describe truth in *The Drama of Doctrine: A Canonical-Linguistic Approach to Christian Theology* (Louisville: Westminster John Knox, 2005), 419–21. Vanhoozer, however, maintains more interest in traditional conceptions of propositional truth than I do.

40. *Aleitheia* is the Greek word translated into English as "truth." It literally refers to something uncovered, not hidden, or made evident. Cf. Oliver Davies, *A Theology of Compassion: Metaphysics of Difference and the Renewal of Tradition* (Grand Rapids: Eerdmans, 2001), 278.

41. Commenting on Kierkegaard's view of truth, Emmanuel Levinas states, "Belief stands in the midst of this conflict between presence and absence—a conflict

takes the form of a struggle against *untruth*, against everything that is soul-destroying and unedifying and that sets itself up against the knowledge of God in Jesus Christ—in our lives, in our communities, and in the world—as we establish a community that manifests the gospel truth. In this way Christian truth stands as an offense to us in our secular condition and often runs counter to our staid interpretations of the world that are based on our empirical observations and rational calculations. Christians, quite literally, are to display another reality and an alternative way of living in and ordering our world—one structured by the message of the crucified and risen Christ and displays the presence and reality of the Holy Spirit. It is a reality shaped by cross and resurrection.

The sense in which Christian truth claims can be verified is the degree to which they are true of *us*—those who believe—both in our corporate and individual lives. The proof of Christian truth does not depend upon a rational apologetic procedure but on the witness of Christians—our full testimony to the truth that edifies us and builds us up. The character and quality of our lives together are a witness that we have been built up and shaped by the truths we confess. This confession involves placing our entire lives on the line, confessing with our words and our lives the truth of God in Jesus Christ and putting ourselves at the disposal of those to whom we witness (Marcel). Vanhoozer notes that the Greek term for one who testifies is *martyr*, which includes both the act of "giving witness" and that of "giving one's life" for the truth.[42] In a truly Kierkegaardian spirit, he goes on to argue that what is ultimately required to stake a theological truth

which remains forever irreconcilable, an open wound, unstaunchable bleeding. But this failure to synthesize is not an intellectual deficiency. It is exactly appropriate to the new mode of truth: the suffering and humbling of truth are not an accident, an external contingency. They are part of its essence as truth; in a way, part of its divinity." "Existence and Ethics," in *Kierkegaard: A Critical Reader*, ed. Jonathan Rée and Jane Chamberlain (Oxford: Blackwell, 1998), 29.

42. Vanhoozer, *First Theology*, 351. Eagleton helpfully distinguishes between a martyr's death and a suicide: "The martyr yields up his or her most precious possession, but would prefer not to; the suicide, by contrast, is glad to be rid of a life that has become an unbearable burden. . . . The word 'martyr' means 'witness'; and what he or she bears witness to is a principle without which it may not be worth living in the first place. In this sense, the martyr's death testifies to the value of life, not to its unimportance." *Faith, Reason, and Revolution*, 26.

claim is *martyrdom*, "for it is the whole speech act of testifying, not only the proposition, that ultimately communicates truth claims about the way of wisdom."[43] The martyr's witness, as one who stakes one's life on the truths by which one has been edified, enables those of us who receive it to imagine a truth bigger than our own lives—one for which we could live and die—and it presents us with an opportunity to make that truth our own. This sort of witness, I contend, creates the conditions for the intelligibility of the truths of the Christian gospel by publically displaying a life or a way of being in which its claims make sense—a life that can *only* be made sense of in terms of those claims.

Conclusion

One of my aims in this chapter has been to redescribe truth from the perspective of subjectivity so that it is immune from the charge of arbitrariness, relativism, or denial of objectivity (or what passes for that). If a reader is tempted to think this way about what I have said, the reader has misread me entirely. The express aim of my redescription is to move us past the modern split between objectivity and subjectivity that forces us to choose one or the other. To be sure, I have emphasized subjectivity over objectivity as the *means* of acquiring truth, and even as giving us a special insight into the nature of truth for humans, but that is not to deny all senses of objectivity. My focus on subjectivity is to resituate objectivity so that we may have both together.

This unity of objectivity and subjectivity is what makes Luther's dramatic formula "Here I stand" emblematic of edifying truth and paradigmatic for Christian truth-telling. As Kierkegaard notes, witnesses are Christians whose proclamation of the gospel starts with their lives.[44] The act of witness *is* the unity of the inner and the outer, subjectivity and objectivity, the public and the private. It is the outward

43. Vanhoozer, *First Theology*, 351.
44. "What is a witness? A witness is a person who directly demonstrates the truth of the doctrine he proclaims—directly, yes, in part by its being truth in him and blessedness, in part by volunteering his personal self and saying: Now see if you can force me to deny this doctrine." Søren Kierkegaard, *Søren Kierkegaard's Journals*

sign of the inward truth of the gospel that contains the light of Christ
in the clay jars of our words and our actions.

But we must not lose sight of the fundamentally aporetic character of the truths to which we witness. Luther in his confession and
Augustine in his passion for truth both teach us that we never possess
the truth for and by ourselves; rather, we are to be possessed *by* the
Truth (together with others). For all of the directness of witness, it
retains its basic and ironic indirectness. The faithful expression of
Christian witness comes in the form of both word and deed (and *only*
in this bivalent form). We can never show the light of Christ and the
truths that edify us *except* through our words and actions—and in
an important sense these truths do not exist for us or those to whom
we witness apart from our full testimony. We will not have the truths
that edify us, nor will we be a witness to them, apart from our fully
assuming them and living so that they shape our words and actions.
This means that the gospel truth ultimately takes the form of a community that displays the gospel truth and makes it possible to imagine
a world in which they exist.

Therefore, we may also characterize gospel truth as *victorious*
truth that overcomes the world, but this victory is eschatological and
future-oriented so that *in this world* it is always an overcoming truth,
always an on-the-way-to-victory truth. It is never a triumphant, sovereign truth that rules and reigns here and now with full and complete
presence. To be eschatological is to be hopeful; it is to be oriented
toward things that are yet to come. The contingent, second-order,
contextual truths of the gospel we come to know and are shaped by
lack the full, objective presence that is the goal of epistemological
inquiry. I believe Stanley Grenz and John Franke are trying to capture
something of this notion of truth in relation to Christian theology
with their emphasis on "eschatological realism."[45] When they say that
Christian language shapes reality by the power of the Holy Spirit
in light of God's future, I do not understand them as proposing yet
another metaphysical thesis nor even as making a statement about

---

and Papers, 7 vols., ed. and trans. Howard V. Hong and Edna H. Hong, assisted by
Gregor Malantschuk (Bloomington, IN: Indiana University Press, 1967–78), §4967.

45. Stanley J. Grenz and John R. Franke, *Beyond Foundationalism: Shaping
Theology in a Postmodern Context* (Louisville: Westminster John Knox, 2001), 272.

the power of language. Instead, I find the importance of their woɪ.
is in the attention they call to the necessary role faith plays in our
witness to gospel truth. If "reality" or Truth does not lie in the world
of sense perception but with "God's eschatological will for creation,"
our witness is decidedly prophetic, and human reason of itself cannot
grasp what is really real. Prophetic witness is not (just) to "objective"
realities but to a world and reality that is on its way to becoming
present here, now. We witness to truths that lack full presence but
are such that, as they edify us, they bring us further into the reality
of God's kingdom that is coming here on earth, where God's will is
done as it is in heaven. These are truths that transform how we live
here and now in our everyday practices, and shape us into the kinds
of persons who are in Truth's possession.

This brings me to an interesting point, as I am able now to turn to
another one of the traits of prophetic speech that ought to characterize Christian witness—namely, its *occasional* character. Prophetic
speech has a specific audience in mind. The prophet is preaching,
you will recall, to persons and has a word tailored to them and their
situation. In the same way, Christian witness does not proclaim a
set of timeless and necessary truths. To *this* person or audience
prophetic witness presents *this* truth that can be edifying for them.
The goal of witness is always to introduce the one who *is* Truth into
the present context in which the witness speaks and lives. Prophetic
speech is not universally prophetic.[46] Addressed to others outside
the situation and specific context of the audience, prophetic witness may be superfluous and even unedifying—and to that extent
untrue, in my sense. But proclaimed at the opportune time, to the
right audience, and in the proper way, witness circumscribes truths
that are suited to its hearers and can be edifying for them. Witness,
then, does not start from some religiously neutral vantage point,
or with arguments that everyone finds to be rational. According to
the picture I have sketched, reason and truth are *always* situated
in some social context, and it is always from a particular place in
life—along with all the assumptions, presuppositions, and various

46. Merold Westphal, *Kierkegaard's Critique of Reason and Society* (University
Park, PA: Pennsylvania State University Press, 1991), 14.

practices and vocabularies we use in them—that we apprehend and think about truth.

Another way to describe the occasionalism of prophetic witness is to say that it has no interest in providing universal reasons for belief or faith that have rational appeal across all the contexts of human life. There is no objective piece of evidence or argument that conclusively verifies Christian truth claims because by nature they are not objective entities. This does not mean we have no reasons for belief or we cannot reason about faith. We can, as Vanhoozer has said, "verify or corroborate biblical wisdom in situations where, in the light of a Christian vision of the whole, we are able to act well."[47] However, I insist the reasons for faith always remain *personal* to a significant degree and are only potentially universal, objectively speaking. On the one hand, this opens up space for my witness to be a genuine attestation to truth that hopes to be in the truth, while on the other hand, it involves genuine concern for the other that precipitates a personal relationship. When truth is viewed this way, as Ricoeur so eloquently describes, it no longer dehumanizes and divides us from others, but is something illuminating and winsome that makes genuine relationships possible:

> The truth, not only formal and abstract, but actual and concrete, ceases to be asserted in a Promethean act of taking a position on the self by the self and of adequation of the self to the self. The truth is rather the lighted place in which it is possible to continue to live and to think. And to think *with* our very opponents themselves, without allowing the totality which contains us ever to become a knowledge about which we can overestimate ourselves and become arrogant.[48]

All of this is bound to produce apoplexy for anyone committed to a modern, objective approach to truth who insists truth requires a metaphysics. Whatever makes statements true in the contexts we make them, and however they come to edify us in and through the concrete practices of our everyday lives, is not something objectively

47. Vanhoozer, *First Theology*, 349.
48. Paul Ricoeur, "Preface: A Response to My Friends and Critics," in *Studies in the Philosophy of Paul Ricoeur*, ed. Charles E. Reagan (Athens, OH: Ohio University Press, 1979).

visible to an abstract theory. But as Terry Eagleton reminds us, faith for Christians is a *gift* and this means Christians are not in conscious possession of all the reasons for their beliefs.[49] There is a kind of practical reason at work, so that I can come to see how believing makes good sense, but this, at best, works in reverse as a type of retrospective justification of what we affirm. I may reflect back on belief and understand the kind of sense it makes, but the reasons for my faith are never apart from that faith, and their justifications do not function to ground faith objectively antecedent to belief. Objectively, Christian belief is always a wager.

We might say, then, that witness creates the conditions for rational engagement with the gospel across different language games. It functions as what Stanley Hauerwas describes as "the condition necessary to begin argument."[50] Objectively, Luther's "Here I stand" did not settle much at all (if anything) but instead initiated a new conversation about faith and how it is to be understood; it produced new conditions for edification. Witness presents a particular perspective or world and challenges its audience to consider it seriously—to look at it closely, to try it on and work out its meaning in one's own life. The act of testimony or attestation therefore provides the starting point for genuine dialogue and effective apologetic engagement. It invites unbelievers to come and measure the worth of our words by our lives, and to measure their own lives by the worth of our words. Witness does not *end* arguments, but it does determine the kind of arguments we make and the shape of our apologetic dialogues. It invites others to see the world in a different light and creates a sphere of rationality distinctive to its content.

I have gone to some lengths to emphasize that my view of truth is agonistic—it is a struggle and a process to be in the truth, not a rational calculation or quick perception. As I have noted, this struggle is not just private but also public, and can be articulated in terms of its inherently ethical and political dimensions. In chapter 5 I turn to a description of the politics of witness.

49. Eagleton, *Faith, Reason, and Revolution*, 138.
50. Stanley Hauerwas, *With the Grain of the Universe: The Church's Witness and Natural Theology* (Grand Rapids: Brazos, 2001), 207.

5

The Politics of Witness

If the believer has any duty at all, it is to become aware
of all that is within him of the non-believer.

Gabriel Marcel

The *rejectability* of the gospel is ironically what prevents
it from becoming mere propaganda. Consequently, the
Good News cannot be fully understood as good *news*
unless the gospel is offered in noncoercive ways.

Brad J. Kallenberg

M abiala Kenzo is a Congolese-Canadian theologian. After
Kenzo gave a lecture on the different ways Jesus is portrayed
in African theology to a group of faculty and students at an evangelical Christian college, a student asked him a question about the
orthodox confessions of Christianity. The question expressed concern
about whether Kenzo thought Africans should first affirm the Chal-
cedonian formula regarding Jesus's two natures before appropriating
their own cultural symbols and categories to understand who Jesus is.
Kenzo responded to the student's query with a question of his own:

"Do I, as an African, have *first* to study and learn Greek philosophy and master its conceptual categories [so he can understand what the orthodox creeds really mean] *before* I can convert to Christianity and believe in Jesus?"

Behind Kenzo's response, I am sure, is a childhood memory he has of watching his father, a respected man in their community, being "naturalized" by the Belgian Congo authorities, so that his father could be considered a citizen of his own country and be able to travel freely within the Congo, hold an official job, and get a passport. This process involved two Belgian officials visiting Kenzo's home to observe, among other things, the family eat a meal at a Western-style table, on chairs, with knives and forks, and with proper table etiquette—instead of eating on the ground and using their fingers after the African customs. After the meal, Kenzo recalls the final test his father had to undergo in order to pass muster. One of the officials remained in the kitchen while the other officer took his father into the living room, where they were to have a conversation in French, loud enough to be heard from the kitchen. If the officer in the kitchen was unable to tell who was speaking because the accents were so uniformly Belgian, then naturalization would be granted and Kenzo's father would receive a matriculation card to become a legal citizen. The obvious assumption underlying this process is that indigenous Africans in the Belgian Congo needed to be "civilized"—literally made into civil entities—and Westernized in order to be full citizens of their country.[1]

Here's my question: Is there a connection between Christian witness and Western colonization of the two-thirds world? Is witnessing to the gospel something akin to naturalizing someone in colonial Africa? As a Christian witness, am I called to be an apostle of Western (and *white*) values—or some other specific set of conceptual and linguistic formulations that give expression to the dominant cultural expression of Christianity? Is my goal as a witness to convert people from other

1. As Kenzo explained to me, the story I report was part of the process for a Congolese to become an "evolué." In Congo in the 1950s, when Congolese were finally allowed to travel overseas, the Belgian created two categories of Congolese. The "evolues" or the "evolved" on the one hand and the "indigenes" or the "indigenous" on the other. Only the "evolués" who held the famous matriculation card could eat in white men's restaurants or have a beer in a white men's pub, or travel abroad.

cultures to the thought forms of Western culture and to approximate Western, European Christian behavior as best they can?

And how does one in circumstances like Kenzo's in colonial Africa receive the Christian gospel—the Good News of Jesus—so that it actually is *good news*? How do they hear that God in Jesus was enfleshed and became *just like them* so that they might know God and the love of God and be in the truth?[2] Do they need to hear an elaborate defense of the Western theological concepts and categories? Or do they need a gospel witness that comes to them in and through their own cultural categories and ways of making sense of the world?

One might ask the same questions regarding the indigenous peoples of North America, particularly those in my home country of Canada, whose children were taken from them forcibly and placed in government residential schools. In these schools their native languages and cultures were taken from them programmatically. And this happened, often, in collaboration with the Christian church, which ran many of the residential schools.

So how do First Nations persons in *these* circumstances, with this history and these experiences, hear the story of Jesus in a way that builds them up and is true *for them*—so that they do not hear a story that justifies injustice and oppression, but one that is good news *for them*, in all their particularity? We could multiply the examples to include all those ethnic people groups who have been marginalized and oppressed by the dominant, mainstream values of societies that have professed to be Christian, or those individuals and groups that have been abused specifically by the church and other church-sanctioned groups. There are many, many such examples from around the world.

To be sure, these concerns regarding colonial and post-colonial Christian witness have hardly gone unnoticed.[3] However, their connection

2. As will become clear in what follows, this is an extreme adumbration of the Christian gospel, which at very least must also be spelled out in terms of the death and resurrection of Jesus—the "Christ event"—in addition to his life. As I understand it, this further means the confession of God as triune who is revealed to us in Jesus. But the Christian gospel is not *less* than incarnation.

3. For just a few of many examples, see Andrew F. Walls, *The Missionary Movement in Christian History: Studies in the Transformation of Faith* (Maryknoll, NY: Orbis, 1969); Lamin O. Sanneh, *Whose Religion Is Christianity? The Gospel Beyond*

to Christian apologetics is usually overlooked. So in this chapter I use them to provoke the questions of the ethical and political dimensions of apologetics itself. One might get the impression from the emphasis in modern apologetics on objective truth that one could never be wrong to use an argument that is valid, sound, and has a true conclusion.[4] However, one of the obvious results of the way I have been talking about truth and witness is that an ethics of witness follows from the ethical nature of belief and truth. And from that must follow a *politics*.[5] But this link from an ethics of belief to witness, and then from an ethics of witness to a politics of witness, will not be immediately apparent unless we keep in mind my earlier insistence that edification is not a private event. Prophetic witness is a personal act that gives full expression to the individual, but does this in such a way that it never leads to privatization.[6] So in this chapter I try to sketch out what the social dimensions of witness look like when edification is taken to be the primary act of witness.

My central claim in this chapter runs something like this: When our concern is with *how* we believe, not only *what* we believe, and when being in the truth is just as important as possessing it, then our Christian witness must be such that it is edifying to those who receive our witness. Our passion for the truth is connected as much to the form our witness takes and how it is received, as it is to the content of that to which we witness. Because the truth we proclaim is not merely objective content that needs to be downloaded and saved

---

the *West* (Grand Rapids: Eerdmans, 2003); Carl Raschke, *GloboChrist: The Great Commission Takes a Postmodern Turn* (Grand Rapids: Baker Academic, 2008); Marion Grau, *Rethinking Mission in the Postcolony: Salvation, Society, and Subversion* (London: T&T Clark, 2011); and Jonathan Ingleby, *Beyond Empire: Postcolonialism and Mission in a Global Context* (Central Milton Keynes, UK: AuthorHouse, 2010).

4. I remember, for example, listening to a rather well-known apologist tell a story over supper to a group of his equally well-known apologist friends at an annual conference about a debate he had recently had with a feminist atheist over issues in bioethics. She apparently objected, at one point, to the male perspective from which his arguments for Christianity were coming. The table roared with laughter as he related his response to her: "Lady, arguments don't have penises!"

5. This is not a new idea, nor is it unique to me. Merold Westphal has been arguing for a similar reading of Kierkegaard since the 1970s. See Merold Westphal, *Kierkegaard's Critique of Reason and Society* (University Park, PA: Pennsylvania State University Press, 1991).

6. Cf. Kevin J. Vanhoozer, *First Theology: God, Scripture and Hermeneutics* (Downers Grove, IL: InterVarsity, 2002), 363.

onto a mainframe, it also cannot be communicated in a manner that
diminishes a person in any way. That which reduces another person
cannot be the truth that comes from Jesus Christ. Thus, as I suggested
in chapter 3, our personal passion for the truth takes communal form
and becomes a politics. The reasons we give for faith and the truths
we defend are connected to an entire way of imagining the world that
is caught up with how we act and believe together in our society or
community. This means that whenever I take up an argument or make
an assertion about anything, I am in fact implicitly defending and
asserting the social imaginary in which they make sense.

Christian witness, then, must be both personal *and* concerned
with public accountability. It requires a community—a *church* in
particular[7]—in which truthful speech is made evident by the quality
and character of their practices and life together. Furthermore, as
we shall see below, a prophetic witness is also political in the more
profound sense of bringing it into conflict with "the powers that be"
or "the established order," as I have referred to it. To confess the
Christian gospel and to be edified by it is at the same time to be called
into a distinct way of being with others that constitutes the church as
God's people—with "power, purpose, and polity."[8] And so our ethics
of truth turns out also to require a politics of truth.

The Ethics of Witness

Not lying far beneath the surface of my skeptical thesis about modern
apologetics is an ethical critique of modern objectivism that goes
along with the ethics of belief I introduced earlier. By "objectivism,"
here, I mean the epistemological thesis that the most important realities are captured objectively in propositions as "objective truths." A
crucial plank in my description of truth is the conviction that, in the
sense most important to the Christian gospel, truth can *only* edify—it

7. Outlining a theology of the church is not one of my goals here, but I trust
it suffices to say that I understand the church as a unique community of subjects
indwelled and called into being as a people by the Holy Spirit through their common
confession of Jesus Messiah as Lord.

8. Douglas Harink, *Paul among the Postliberals: Pauline Theology beyond Christendom and Modernity* (Grand Rapids: Brazos, 2003), 245.

cannot tear down. That is, if some piece of communication—whether an argument or a propositional assertion—is not edifying, it is not the truth. A kind of reverse alchemy takes place when some piece of objectively agreed-upon information is used to do something violent or unethical to another person. The high-grade bullion of truth is thereby rendered into something leaden, worthless, and even toxic— and so fails to be the truth in the sense I use it here.

C. S. Lewis, it would seem, gets at something close to this point in his children's story *The Last Battle*, when the character Emeth (Hebrew: אמת, "truth") arrives in Aslan's country at the end of his life and is finally confronted by Aslan. Emeth has spent his entire life despising Aslan and worshipping Tash, the god of Narnia's enemies and the enemy of Aslan. Emeth is therefore justifiably confused at his welcome by Aslan and asks if Aslan and Tash really are one and the same god, just as the false prophet had said. Aslan replies that it is not because they are the same, but because they are *opposites*, that Emeth finds himself welcomed in Aslan's country (i.e., in the Truth; Truth's final destination). "For I and he are of such different kinds," Aslan reasons, "that no service which is vile can be done to me, and none which is not vile can be done to him."[9] Those who swear by Tash and keep their oath "for the oath's sake" have in truth sworn by *Aslan* and are rewarded by him. And likewise, Aslan continues, if anyone does a cruelty in Aslan's name, it is not Aslan who is being served, even though his name is used, but Tash. The service rendered is not to the Truth (Aslan) but to that which is false (Tash).

Here, in a nutshell, is the basic move from an ethics of belief to an ethics of witness. Underlying Lewis's point in the above passage is a Kierkegaardian insistence that *how* we say or believe something is as important as *what* we say or believe. The veracity of Emeth's beliefs about his god is linked to *how* he confesses them, and only secondarily related to what exactly Emeth professes. It is not that Lewis erases all difference between conflicting affirmations—as if *what* is the case does not matter at all. Aslan unequivocally denies that he is the same as Tash and asserts that saying so is not correct. Rather, taken purely "objectively," what Emeth professes does not

9. C. S. Lewis, *The Last Battle* (New York: MacMillan, 1956), 165.

get at what is really important to being in Truth's way. Thus, it is not possible either, Aslan insists, to proclaim truth in an unedifying or "vile" way. When one does so, one is proclaiming something false, a pseudo-gospel, and is serving the Father of Lies. The lesson in this for Christian witness is that I cannot use the objective truths of Christianity to tear down others and think that I am thereby communicating the truth of the gospel.

This point might also be made by noting that speaking is itself a kind of action. Oxford philosopher John Austin makes the fairly obvious—but provocative—observation that we use the words we speak to perform a wide range of actions and not just to refer to things.[10] What our words *mean*, then, is not a simple matter of checking the dictionary and diagramming the sentences for their grammar. For example, I might say to someone, "Open the door," because I am hot and want to cool down. But I may also ask someone to "Open the door" because I want to show a friend how my dog does neat tricks; or maybe I want my daughter, who closed the door on her younger sister, to be nice to her sister. Examining the common definitions of the words *open*, *the*, and *door*, along with the grammar of "Open the door," will not tell you much about any of the ways I am actually *using* the sentence in a given speech act.

This means, furthermore, that speaking has an ethical dimension that goes beyond the question of whether the content of what I say is objectively true or factually accurate. Whenever I speak, I am performing an action that may be wrong or morally objectionable regardless of the propositional content of what I say. I can use the words "Jesus is Lord," for instance, to make someone else feel unspiritual by comparison, rather than to declare the lordship of Christ.[11]

10. J. L. Austin, *How to Do Things with Words* (Oxford: Oxford University Press, 1962). Readers will recognize this as the central insight of the speech-act theory of language that followed from Austin's work.
11. Vanhoozer asks us to consider the simple act of saying "Jesus is Lord." He explains that I could be doing any one (or more) of seven things by saying that sentence: (1) I could be simply making vocal sounds—maybe warming up for a speech; (2) I could be showing friends how well I can imitate a French accent; (3) I could simply be repeating a sentence someone else said to me—"Jesus is Lord"; (4) I could be confessing that Jesus is Lord; (5) I could be witnessing to my next door neighbor and telling her that Jesus is Lord; (6) I could be offering an explanation to someone

The point is that I will not appreciate completely (or even basically) what is happening when someone says the sentence "Jesus is Lord" merely by studying its constituent grammatical and lexical parts. If I am to understand how "Jesus is Lord" is being used in any given speech situation, it will require much more in-depth attention to the wider context in which the sentence is uttered and *how* it is being used—what language game is being played and why, who the actors are and what they have at stake in the conversation. And this will necessarily involve treating my words as if they are communication between *persons*, each of whom have goals and desires they bring to the speech situation and are a constituent part of it.

But from this also follows the insight that *arguments* are used to do things too. They are not just naked pieces of reasoning that present us with the untarnished and objective truth about a matter. Arguments, in fact, do not even exist as such apart from humans who make them and use them.[12] And I may use valid arguments to perform a wide range of actions: to protect my dignity, to rebut some claim about the incoherence of Christian doctrine, to make someone else feel silly, to hide my real thoughts, to maintain control of a situation, to protect someone else from wrong thoughts, to avoid talking about my feelings, to fool someone into believing something I believe to be false, to demonstrate my intellectual superiority over someone, and so on. The number of things I can do with an argument is exhausted only by my lack of creativity.

So, just like other speech actions, arguments are ethical entities as well. Arguments that in every other objectively determinate way are good, true, valid, or plausible can be used to perform reprehensible actions, much in the same way I might say "Jesus is Lord" in order to make someone else feel small. This means that the responsibilities I

---

as to why my cancer suddenly went into remission; or (7) I could be making someone else feel unspiritual by comparison. There are also dozens of other things we could be doing with that sentence. *First Theology*, 172.

12. Since the 1960s, George I. Mavrodes has argued that even formal soundness for an argument is person-relative in that an argument counts as sound only if some person is able rationally to acknowledge it as such and what each person rationally believes is different. So some arguments may be formally sound to one person and not to another. *Belief in God: A Study in the Epistemology of Religion* (Washington, DC: University Press of America, 1970), 40–41.

have when I make an argument (just as whenever I speak) go beyond a simple evaluation of whether or not my argument achieved the conditions for formal soundness or has an objectively "true" conclusion. When I assume, with the modern epistemological paradigm, that human beings are essentially epistemological entities—"things that think"—whose most basic need is to accept the right propositions, then it is easy and perhaps even natural to assume that the best thing I can do for an unbeliever is to reason with them militantly in such a way as to win the argument and force my conclusion. It is "true," after all, and I am right! My focus will be on *what* I argue about—the conclusions and propositions, the facts and the evidence to support them, and whether my opponent and I believe them—not *how* I engage another *person*. And, in the end, it will be difficult to escape the conclusion that my primary objective in an apologetic encounter is winning the argument. I may further believe people with beliefs different than mine are morally suspect, since there might not be another explanation for why they refuse to accept my rational conclusions. So the degree to which my driving concern is the communication of objective truths is also the degree to which I treat unbelievers in terms of objective knowledge and essentially lose the ability to be *responsive* to them as persons.[13]

Once again Gabriel Marcel is helpful. He distinguishes between the different forms of address we use with others that correspond to our contrasting emphases on objectivity or subjectivity. *Coercion* is the form our interaction with others takes when our main concern is with the possession of objective truth—whether we have it, whether they have it, and so forth.[14] I attempt to coerce someone in this sense

13. Gabriel Marcel, *Creative Fidelity*, trans. Robert Rosthal (New York: The Noonday Press, 1964), 50–52.
14. Apologist Paul D. Feinberg notes that "a demonstrably sound argument is *coercive* in the sense that anyone who wants to retain rationality must accept the argument" (my emphasis). "Cumulative Case Apologetics," in *Five Views on Apologetics*, ed. Steven B. Cowan (Grand Rapids: Zondervan, 2000), 148. Feinberg refers us to the "fine discussion" in John Hick, *Arguments for God's Existence* (New York: Seabury, 1971), vii–xiii, to bolster his point. Feinberg himself does not think that any such arguments for God's existence or the truth of Christianity exist, but goes on to make a "cumulative case" for Christian belief that, while not absolutely coercive in the sense of closing all the rational doors available to one, is designed nonetheless

whenever I use rational arguments (or just flat assertions of objective truth) in order to compel others (by rational force, intimidation, or authority) to accept my way of understanding and speaking about the world (or God, etc.), without regard to their personal desires or volition. This sort of militancy often attaches to the pursuit of objective truth because of the perception that truth is indifferent to persons and a perceived need to demonstrate one's beliefs indeed *are* the objective truth that appears to be connected to the fixation on objectivity. The modern emphasis on possessing and demonstrating for oneself that one's beliefs are objectively true may create a great deal of anxiety for me that can often be alleviated only by requiring that everyone else agrees with me.[15] To appropriate a metaphor: When my emphasis is on objectivity, I should not just attempt to lead a thirsty horse to water; I should *drag* it. And once I have done so, I should do all I can to make them drink—whether they think they want my water or not!

Appeal, on the other hand, is concerned with the more personal question of being in the truth and engages others on the basis of our shared humanity. When I appeal to someone, I remain sensitive to them as a spiritual being, a person, someone who—like me—has a project or task to be in truth. When I appeal to someone, then, I ask them to believe me because I am interested in what interests them and I understand how they see the world. I remain open to the person and acknowledge their presence as an other, *as having a face*—a face that calls me, summons me, implores me to acknowledge their presence *as such*. By contrast, coercion perpetuates the self-preoccupation of objectivity. It always sees the world from *its* vantage point and as

___

to back one into a corner whose only escape is to opt for a door that is less than the best rational alternative.

15. The ethos of modernity tends to produce a fixation on mastery and control that is a product of the tension between the genius and the crowd described earlier. Richard J. Bernstein gives this phenomenon a name. He observes that the objectivism of the modern epistemological paradigm generates a nascent anxiety for moderns that stems from the need to avoid the epistemological chaos of a relativistic skepticism in which nothing is determinately true or known for certain. Bernstein calls this "Cartesian anxiety" after the seventeenth-century philosopher René Descartes. *Beyond Objectivism and Relativism: Science, Hermeneutics, and Praxis* (Philadelphia: University of Pennsylvania Press, 1983), 16–20.

existing *for it*, and objectifies others from this vantage point, along with the rest of the world.

Coercion, then, is a subtle form of violence against another person. With coercion I use reason and argumentation almost as a cudgel to bend someone's mind to my will. Evidence and arguments become a way for me to shield myself simultaneously from genuine personal engagement and self-examination in the encounter with the other, and to remove any threat to my beliefs and self-perception by transforming the other into my likeness. So not only does apologetic coercion reduce others in our eyes, but if successful, it also diminishes others in their own eyes. Marcel elaborates:

> The individual who tries to coerce us, forgets or pretends to forget that we are [humans]; insofar as we give in to him, *we cease to be present to ourselves*, for *he alienates us from ourselves.* . . . Appeal, on the other hand, mysteriously restores us to ourselves. Not inevitably, of course, since we can refuse to give ourselves to it.[16]

Rational coercion attempts to leverage others into a position in which they do not wish to be and to accept beliefs they do not see as contributing to their own interests as persons. They are forced to acknowledge priorities and values that are not their own and thus, as Marcel says, are alienated from themselves. And so, when I try to coerce or force unbelievers to accept my Christian witness through cleverly devised apologetic arguments and brilliantly devised pieces of rhetoric, I often compel them to believe me *despite* themselves.

With appeal the reverse is true. It asks others to believe *because* of themselves—their goals, interests, and desires. Accordingly, Marcel describes appeal in terms of "submerging oneself in the life of another person and being forced to see things through his eyes."[17] To appeal to someone, I have to understand how they view their world, what their interests are, and why they do what they do. This requires a deep *sympathy* (Marcel's term) with the things that the individual cares

16. Marcel, *Creative Fidelity*, 51–52 (my emphasis).
17. Ibid., 51. We see a beautiful illustration of this form of witness in the New Testament account of the Samaritan woman's witness after her encounter with Jesus at Jacob's well in John 4:29: "Come and see a man who told me everything I have ever done!" she tells the people of her city. "He cannot be the Messiah, can he?"

about and a concern for their overall well-being. Sympathy—this way of identifying with the interests, cares, and concerns of another person—is an extension of Marcel's concept of disposability described earlier. Sympathetic appeal involves this same mode of being with others in which I place myself at the disposal of the other rather than viewing them as objects in my world. This type of self-identification with others, Marcel believes, is the only way to eliminate the self-obsession that comes with the desire to achieve objective truth. Thus, appeal is a crucial extension of Marcel's ethics of belief, in which I shift from "you belong to me" and I can dispose of you as I choose, to "I belong to you" and *I* am at *your* disposal.[18] The ethics of belief produces an ethics of witness that can be spelled out in terms of appeal.

Notice that this is precisely the sort of stance apostles and prophets take in their proclamation of the gospel. At least this is true of the letters of St. Paul in the New Testament, particularly the first letter to the Corinthians. Paul *appeals* to the Corinthians as his brothers and sisters on the basis of the identity he shares with them in Jesus Christ (1 Cor. 1:10). And he is able to do so because he shares their way of life. Paul lives, works, and worships with the Corinthians[19] and is willing to become "all things to all people" in order that "by all means [he] might save some" (1 Cor. 9:22). Douglas Harink notes that Paul's form of persuasion with the Corinthians is predicated on his coming to them "in weakness and in fear and in much trembling" (1 Cor. 2:3).[20] Though he is adequately trained and equipped to engage them on the basis of his intellectual prowess and persuade them through rational coercion, Paul steadfastly resists any form of persuasion with the Corinthians other than the message of the cross and the power of the Holy Spirit.[21] In a culture that prizes rhetorical brilliance and believes a person is as they speak, Paul risks rejection by appearing weak and refusing to base the power of his message

18. Marcel, *Creative Fidelity*, 40. I discussed this in chap. 3.
19. Acts 18:3–4.
20. Harink, *Paul among the Postliberals*, 247.
21. 1 Cor. 2:1–3. Cf. Harink, *Paul among the Postliberals*, 247. See Ben Witherington III, *Conflict and Community in Corinth: A Socio-Rhetorical Commentary on 1 and 2 Corinthians* (Grand Rapids: Eerdmans, 1995), especially 121–29, for a penetrating treatment of Paul's rhetorical strategy in preaching the gospel to the Corinthians.

on the power of his personality, presentation, or performance.[22] He refuses to place the Corinthians beneath him or treat them as objects at his disposal. Instead, he makes himself vulnerable to them, identifying with them, and relates to them in such a way that he cannot guarantee what their response to his message will be. In Marcel's terms, Paul places himself at the *disposal* of the Corinthians, and he does this precisely because he does not wish to falsify the message he proclaims—"so that the cross of Christ might not be emptied of its power" (1 Cor. 1:17).

The question of *what* I witness to as a Christian, then, is deeply connected to the question of *how* I witness. And as a *Christian* witness, what I am witness to is the gospel of Jesus Christ. This message is a peculiar truth because it testifies to a paradoxical reality: that the power of God is displayed through the suffering and death of Jesus on the cross.[23] For Paul, the gospel of Jesus is indistinguishable from the *life* (and death and resurrection) of Jesus. The gospel is therefore a *way* of being in the world for Paul—a way that, as Harink notes, seeks not its own advantage but that of the other, and according to which we each become servants of the other as a community of mutual upbuilding.[24] Jesus himself gives formal content to this way of life by summarizing the entire law in the command, love God by loving your neighbor (Matt. 22:37–39). And for Paul, this means "the only thing that counts [for anything] is faith working through love" (Gal. 5:6). Paul does not ground his proclamation of the gospel in his own power and resources but positions himself so that his weakness is evident and the power of God is magnified. In this way, Paul's witness is shaped in very concrete and practical ways by the truth that he proclaims.

The bottom line in all this for Christian witness is that my attempts to coerce my neighbor rationally demonstrate that I really do not love my neighbor as I love myself, and that the form of my witness does not embody the gospel truth. I do not treat my neighbor's edification as critical to my own, and I argue or attempt to persuade out of my own strength rather than the power of Christ in me. This is

22. Cf. Witherington, *Conflict and Community in Corinth*, 123–24.
23. Cf. 1 Cor. 1:18: "For the message about the cross is foolishness to those who are perishing, but to us who are being saved it is the power of God."
24. Harink, *Paul among the Postliberals*, 247.

then doubly problematic for the Christian witness who engages in rational coercion, because *the gospel truth itself* appears to demand that my witness be rejected. As we already saw, being a witness to the truth means taking a stand against everything that is untruth and unedifying. But it also means bearing witness to the strength of Christ in and through our own weakness. When Christians use arguments as a means of coercion—regardless of their Christian propositional content—those arguments are unedifying and do not witness to the truth. Inasmuch as modern apologetics takes the objective truth of the Christian message as its principal concern, and makes rational demonstration of these objective truths its primary goal, it will be virtually impossible to witness to the truth of the gospel as I have described it. Such a witness has a difficult time edifying because its mode of engagement tends toward violent disregard for the subjectivity of those to whom it is addressed.

Apologetic Violence

Prophetic witness, we may say then, is nonviolent and noncoercive—it is *person-preserving*. That is, it avoids what I have called apologetic violence. There are two dangers here—one rather immediate and obvious, the other more indirect and difficult to detect. The first type of apologetic violence is a kind of rhetorical violence[25] that occurs whenever a witness is indifferent to others as *persons* and treats them "objectively," as objects defined by their intellectual positions on Christian doctrine or as representatives of certain social subcategories. This does not rule out vigorous disagreement with (or rigorous critique of) someone's beliefs or worldview or their reasons for belief; as I stated earlier, a prophetic witness is bound to clash with the world, and it takes a stand against untruth. Rather, I commit this first kind of apologetic violence when I treat those without my faith *en masse* under a universal category, such as "unbeliever," so

---

25. Rhetorical violence here does not mean that it is illusory or merely assumed, but rather it is a kind of violence we perform through our acts of persuasion—our rhetoric. It is to be contrasted with physical violence, which we perform with our bodies, and is a close cousin to emotional abuse (which is contrasted with physical abuse).

that their individual subjectivity is effectively erased or ignored. As we have seen, this happens in apologetic situations when the primary emphasis is on which propositions or beliefs a person is presently holding and what reasons (or epistemological justification) they have for those beliefs.

William Lane Craig seems to recognize this danger as well and cautions budding apologists that apologetics may distract us from presenting the gospel, so that our focus is "on the argument instead of on the unbeliever." "Remember," he warns, "our aim in evangelism is always to present Christ."[26] This elicits a worry, though: Why is the category Craig uses to identify the major focus of apologetic interest "the unbeliever" and not the *person*? On closer examination, there is a fairly pronounced tension between Craig's admonition that the goal of witness is to "present Christ," his insistence that the truth of Christianity (Christ himself?) is packaged objectively in propositions, and his warning regarding the danger of focusing on arguments. Given Craig's method and approach, what does it mean to focus on "the unbeliever" when one presents the gospel? Craig's concept of Christian witness boils down to the transmission of specific propositions regarding God, Jesus Christ, self, and the world to "the unbeliever" so "the unbeliever" may rationally come to accept them. So how does one *not* focus on the argument while doing this? The primary apologetic and evangelistic goal here is to change "the unbeliever's" mind rather than edify the person.[27] Craig's general apologetic approach and the language he uses convey the impression that the focus of Craig's apologetics is less on *the person* and their *edification* and more on the individual's *beliefs* and their *justification*. This sort of concern for "the unbeliever" is

26. William Lane Craig, *Reasonable Faith: Christian Truth and Apologetics*, 3rd ed. (Wheaton: Crossway, 2008), 57. "The unbeliever," in fact, is Craig's primary term of reference for those to whom one witnesses, and he has a short section in *Reasonable Faith* titled "The Unbeliever" (46–47).

27. Of course, edification and changing one's mind are not mutually exclusive. The issue is one of priority here. Perhaps I could put it this way: Craig appears to believe that in evangelism and apologetics the best, most edifying thing he can do for "the unbeliever" is to change their mind. My emphasis on edification means that my interest is on building up the other person and helping them meet Jesus as I have done. No doubt this will result in a radical change of mind, but it will more importantly involve a change in practices and values as well. This may be a very long process, however, and will always be set in the context of my overall concern for the person.

reminiscent of the sales manager who reminds her sales representatives that it is all about "the customer," while making it clear that this is not meant to extend to the customer's personal life—and even more to the customer's financial well-being, which might well be better off without the salesperson's "concern." For all practical purposes, then, "the unbeliever" is a "faceless" entity who is defined by unbelief.

Perhaps I need to explain this concept of "facelessness" further. I am following Emmanuel Levinas when he identifies "the face" as the mysterious phenomenon that indicates a human being is present.[28] The face of the other, Levinas claims, always points to a reality beyond me that is other than me and can never be mine nor even fully understood. Most important, the face is not an objective, epistemological entity that denotes a mind and signifies beliefs that I am to reason about, justify, and intellectually master, but a hermeneutical phenomenon that speaks to me and calls or summons me to relate to it and to be responsible for it. That is, the face of an other presents me with a presence full of possibilities for personal and distinctly human relationship. To be face*less*, then, is to be anonymous and without being—a *thing* or object, something without a personal and human presence.[29] So when I treat others who do not believe as I do as faceless, I do them a kind of violence.[30]

---

28. "The human being is that which has a face." Emmanuel Levinas, *Totality and Infinity: An Essay on Exteriority*, trans. Alphonso Lingis (Pittsburgh: Duquesne University Press, 1969), 78. I am adopting this part of Levinas's analysis of "the face"—the signification of human being—and not necessarily the full phenomenological package that comes with it.

29. Levinas, *Totality and Infinity*, 139–40. Levinas, no doubt, would prefer to use the term "absolute presence" to describe the face rather than "personal presence" as I do.

30. The question of what counts as violent is both an important and particularly difficult one. I do not presume to provide such an account here, but my inclination is not to "ontologize" violence, as if it has a specific metaphysical essence or presence that is manifest and expressed in every violent context. The approach I favor would be to identify a set of family resemblances between the different ways our concept of violence is used in various contexts and practices—i.e., our language games. I should note, however, that in general my understanding of violence here will allow for good or healthy differentiation and separation—unlike the view taken by Jacques Derrida and John D. Caputo, who believe that predication or naming is itself "originary violence," which is Dallas Willard's fitting terminology in Dallas Willard, "Predication as Originary Violence: A Phenomenological Critique of Derrida's View of Intentionality," in *Working Through Derrida*, ed. Gary B. Madison (Evanston, IL: Northwestern University Press, 1993), 120–36. Cf. Jacques Derrida, *Writing and Difference*, ed. and

I wrong them. I deny their full humanity and attempt to absorb their identity into mine.

In Marcel's terms, treating people this way places them at *my* disposal, so that they exist *for me*. I cease to be responsive to them as fellow persons. When I engage "the unbeliever," I am less concerned with who they are; how their cultural concepts, categories, and symbols function to convey the gospel; where they are in their spiritual journey; or why they believe and think like they do, than I am with whether they acknowledge a specific set of beliefs. And I certainly do not treat them as those through whom the voice of God may speak to me or even as those from whom I may learn or who may inform my life and perspective in some way. They simply are "unbelievers." These might be nuanced into subcategories of unbelievers—such as "pagan," "atheist," "Muslim," or "African" unbelievers—but the main lens through which they are perceived, understood, and related to is that of the "unbeliever," in large measure irrespective of their personal history. The primary focus is on the abstract beliefs a person has (or does not have), and to this degree they are diminished in my eyes as full persons. I take little or no responsibility for their being (or well-being), and their cognitive conversion (a change of mind)—not their edification—is my chief concern.[31]

---

trans. Alan Bass (Chicago: University of Chicago Press, 1978), especially 70–155. I do not consider the mere act of labeling or categorization as inherently or essentially violent, if for no other reason than the fact that understanding violence that way involves ontologizing it. Neither do I believe we must understand violence as a necessary part of dividing and establishing separate identities. Miroslav Volf provides an insightful theological account that contrasts the exclusionary violence of "expulsion, assimilation, or subjugation and the indifference of abandonment" with the proper separation and differentiation established by God in creation, which facilitates the recognition of the other as someone who, in their otherness, is connected to me in a pattern of interdependence. *Exclusion and Embrace: A Theological Exploration of Identity, Otherness, and Reconciliation* (Nashville: Abingdon, 1996), 67. An important attribute of violence as I am using it here is the erasing, ignoring, or nonacknowledgment of the identity of another and of their full status as a fellow human being.

31. It may certainly be the case that conversion to Christianity is an important aim of Christian witness. My point here is regarding, first, the nature of conversion and, second, the reason a Christian witness will be interested in a person's conversion. As regards the latter point, I am saying that conversion will be encouraged by a Christian witness because it is indispensable to being in Christ, and not because the witness is focused (just) on getting the person to have right beliefs. And this is because, as regards the former point, while conversion necessarily involves changing one's mind about a

This approach stands in stark contrast to the prophetic witness of one like the apostle Paul, who, as Douglas Harink notes, "takes a *complex* measure of the other, in contrast to any simple homogenization under one category."[32] Paul engages believers and unbelievers, Jews and Greeks, men and women, slaves and free, all patiently and carefully in terms of their concrete, particular identities within the context of their actual situations. He lives with those to whom he preaches. He eats with them. He works and worships with them. Consequently, his theological categories do not blind him to the particularities of those to whom he witnesses—to the point where Paul does not even think of others in terms of a "universal human condition."[33] Paul's preaching calls the people of the nations not to be conformed to the theological categories he inherited from Jewish orthodoxy (e.g., "circumcision"), but to faithful confession of Jesus as Lord within their cultural forms, whatever they may be.[34] It is as if for Paul, as missiologist Andrew Walls observes, Christianity "has no fixed cultural element" and is therefore "infinitely transferable."[35] For not only *can* the Christian gospel be translated into new cultural and linguistic thought forms, but given the missionary imperative explicit in Paul's letters (and the entire biblical narrative), there is a sense in which the truth of the gospel *requires* this kind of translation: "It is as though

---

great deal of things, this cognitive conversion is not sufficient for full Christian conversion. What is required in conversion is rather a total-person response (beliefs, practices, and dispositions) to the gospel. A change in a person's beliefs is therefore as much the *effect* of conversion as its cause. To repeat, merely changing one's cognitive beliefs is not sufficient to bring about full conversion. Augustine, for example, describes experiencing an intellectual acceptance of Christianity prior to his full (cognitive, bodily, and existential) conversion to Christianity in the sacrament of baptism. See Saint Augustine, *Confessions*, trans. Henry Chadwick (Oxford: Oxford University Press, 1991), 89, 163. For a recent discussion of these issues in conversion that (surprisingly) makes a similar claim, see Andrew Collier, *On Christian Belief: A Defence of a Cognitive Conception of Religious Belief in a Christian Context* (Oxford: Blackwell, 2003), 62–63.

32. Harink, *Paul among the Postliberals*, 248. See also Harink's trenchant discussion on pages 248–54.

33. Harink (ibid., 249) makes this point citing Terence L. Donaldson, *Paul and the Gentiles: Remapping the Apostle's Convictional World* (Minneapolis: Fortress, 1997), 107–64.

34. Cf. Harink, *Paul among the Postliberals*, 252. One might also point to the eschatological vision of the new Jerusalem of Rev. 21:24, where "the nations will walk by its light, and the kings of the earth will bring their glory into it."

35. Walls, *The Missionary Movement in Christian History*, 13, 22.

Christ himself actually grows through the work of mission."[36] Rather than as the faceless unbeliever, then, prophetic Christian witnesses regard those to whom they witness in terms of their full identities as persons—with all the complexities of culture, language, politics, and history (personal and social).

The specific form of Christian prophetic witness, then, is what Paul and the New Testament writers call *agapē* (love), that specifically Christian mode of self-giving love that defines Jesus's command to love one's neighbor as oneself (Matt. 22:39). As Kierkegaard develops it, the Christian concept of "neighbor" is even more radically person-preserving than the above emphasis on "the person" or even "the face" of the other yields.[37] In a parallel move to his genius/apostle distinction, Kierkegaard argues in *Works of Love* that the Christian encounter with others always starts first and foremost with *God*.[38] That is, a genuinely Christian encounter with others does not begin with the face that appears to me but with fear and trembling before God and with the biblical command to love the neighbor. I am confronted first, not with an image (of the face of the other), but with a sound—the *voice of God* by which I am addressed and called into question and that also sets the stage for every other encounter I may have.[39] This

36. Ibid., xvii. This understanding of Paul's witness and his missionary efforts to expand the body of Christ is a crucial extension of Paul's theology of the body of Christ, which includes "Jews and Greeks, slaves or free," "one body" (1 Cor. 12:12–14)—and which he further describes as "the mystery . . . made known to [him] by revelation" (Eph. 3:3) and the basis of his apostleship to the Gentiles (Eph. 1–3, especially 3:1–6).

37. See Søren Kierkegaard, *Works of Love*, ed. and trans. Howard V. Hong and Edna H. Hong (Princeton: Princeton University Press, 1995); especially the First Series, II. B., "You Shall Love the Neighbour," 44–60. Here I am summarizing part of my argument in Myron B. Penner, "Trinity and the Hospitable Cross: Kierkegaard Reads Derrida and Boersma," *Canadian Evangelical Review* 30–31 (2006). For a masterful exposition of Kierkegaard's *Works of Love* along the same lines as mine here, see M. Jamie Ferreira, *Love's Grateful Striving: A Commentary on Kierkegaard's* Works of Love (Oxford: Oxford University Press, 2001). Ferreira very helpfully brings Kierkegaard into dialogue with the work of Levinas throughout her book.

38. Kierkegaard, *Works of Love*, 24–25. One of Kierkegaard's more astounding claims and most penetrating insights in his magisterial *Works of Love* is that our love of the other collapses into yet another form of self-love if it is drawn from our own resources and does not begin with God.

39. Cf. Merold Westphal, *Transcendence and Self-Transcendence: On God and the Soul* (Bloomington, IN: Indiana University Press, 2004), 221.

means that when I experience others on their own terms, in terms of how I see the face,[40] it is very difficult—if not impossible—for me to avoid treating them as existing for me. If I start from the other's appearance to me, Kierkegaard cautions, inevitably I am conscious of the other as existing *for* me, as part of *my* world, no matter how much the countenance of the other escapes my gaze. The neighbor becomes "the *other I*," or one just like me.[41] Beginning with the voice of God, however, opens up the possibility that for me the neighbor is the other *you*—the "*first you*" who exists as a self before God just like me.[42] We might say that for Kierkegaard it is the command of God, the voice of God, that addresses and calls the prophetic witness into being and that gives actual shape to the face of the other as the neighbor—the other "self," who in his or her otherness is just like me. Ironically, then, it is *only* when I love the neighbor *through* God—his Word to us, his call—that others may be loved by me directly and their full personhood preserved.[43]

So the truth to which I witness is at the same time that which edifies me and that which presents me with the neighbor to whom I witness—the one for whom I am infinitely responsible, to whom I have an infinite debt (because it is to *God*), and whose subjectivity I must not violently erase, ignore, or diminish in any way. Love builds

40. For Levinas, the other who appears to me and whose face summons me is never identical to the countenance I see. Levinas, *Totality and Infinity*, 6. So the *appearance* of the other to me in "the face" I take to be Levinas's attempt to designate the appearance of the other to me *on the other's terms*, not mine. Cf. Roger Burggraeve "Violence and the Vulnerable Face of the Other: The Vision of Emmanuel Levinas on Moral Evil and Our Responsibility," *Journal of Social Philosophy* 30 (1999): 29–30.
41. Kierkegaard writes, "In the beloved and the friend, it of course is not the neighbor who is loved, but the *other I*, or the first *I* once again, but more intensely." *Works of Love*, 57.
42. Ibid.
43. Westphal summarizes Kierkegaard's point regarding the command to love the neighbor very well: "So, far from being the condition of the possibility of the neighbor love command, the merely human I and We, along with their horizons of meaning and truth, are the conditions of its impossibility. . . . The command to love my neighbor (law) is not merely or even primarily about my beliefs. It is about my actions, my attitudes, my affections, my very identity. . . . *God is the voice beyond my own who calls me to a life beyond my own through a promise and a command beyond any knowledge or will of my own.*" *Transcendence and Self-Transcendence*, 224.

up, Kierkegaard teaches—it cannot tear down.[44] Consequently, the Christian witness seeks to *win over*, in love, the one to whom he or she witnesses, but not to the witness's own program. Rather than fighting against the "enemy," the witness fights *for* the one with whom the witness is engaged, to whom the witness belongs, and for whom the witness is concerned. But fights? "Against whom?" Kierkegaard asks. Why, against *oneself*! The greatest loss of all in love is that in my exuberance for the truth I crush and destroy the neighbor whom I love, that I cause my neighbor to lose their identity in an objective system of belief that my neighbor neither cares for nor sees as connected to his or her own interests and desires as a person.[45] Therefore, in my appeal to my neighbor I am always careful to fight against all my tendencies to dominate, subjugate, or otherwise coerce my neighbor. In this way, the person-preserving stance of the prophetic witness is a concrete extension of the command to love the neighbor as oneself.

This prophetic stance I am recommending for Christian witness is person-preserving in an ironic way—by grounding all my relations (to self and other) in the Word (or voice) of God. This further means that—as much as Freud, Marx, and Nietzsche, or Foucault, Derrida, and Lyotard—a prophetic witness believes that to a significant degree I am shaped (including my consciousness, beliefs, values, and self-perceptions) by forces beyond my direct control. I am not in full or direct possession of myself. To use New Testament language, the world is an arena in which "principalities," "governments," "thrones," "authorities," "angels," and the "elemental spirits of the universe" act.[46] These powers are material and spiritual and show themselves in concrete behaviors, but they

44. For a beautiful expression of this principle, see the chapter "Love Builds Up," in Kierkegaard, *Works of Love*, 209–24.

45. Kierkegaard writes: "Long, long before the enemy thinks is seeking agreement, the loving one is already in agreement with him; and not only that, no, he has gone over to the enemy's side, is fighting for his cause; even if he does not understand it or is unwilling to understand it, he is working here to bring it to an agreement. See, this can be called a battle of love or a battle in love! . . . to fight *for* the enemy—and against whom? Against oneself." *Works of Love*, 335.

46. Darrell L. Guder, ed., *Missional Church: A Vision for the Sending of the Church in North America* (Grand Rapids: Eerdmans, 1998), 110–11. For the classic treatment of powers in the Bible along the lines I am interpreting them here, see H. Berkhof, *Christ and the Powers*, trans. John Howard Yoder (Scottdale, PA: Herald), 1962. See

also produce an ethos or atmosphere that exerts an influence over attitudes and perceptions regarding the accepted or "normal" way of doing things. Think, as an example, of how national identities—like "the American way"—show up in political rallies, blogs, chat boards, media scrums, newscasts, city council meetings, corporate board meetings, school plays, football games, and so on, and function to frame and form attitudes and beliefs. Capitalism is another example of a power in our (Western) society that shapes a wide range of beliefs and practices, from our attitudes about and perception of money, to how we conduct ourselves politically and fund social institutions (such as schools, cancer research centers, and homeless shelters), to how we organize our homes and think about individuals in our society. These are all examples of how a "power" works. In fact, all of us, St. Paul says, are subject to a complex system of these powers, which are "a multifarious, multilayered, overlapping, interrelated, mutually conditioning set of participations" in social, political, religious, and spiritual realities.[47] We are not in control of these powers and in themselves they are neither wholly good nor wholly evil. They are what constitute us as *subjects*—as those who exist in relation to others, the principal relation being with God, but whose relations always exist against the backdrop of the powers and authorities that provide the context and trajectory for them.[48] And these powers as they presently are configured and exercised under sin and the law are precisely that which the gospel of Jesus Christ is designed to address—as *the* power that overcomes them all.[49] (Only we must always remember that we are speaking of the "power" of a crucified Lord who comes in weakness.) This means that a prophetic

also the work of Walter Wink, particularly *Naming the Powers: The Language of Power in the New Testament* (Philadelphia: Fortress, 1984).

47. Harink, *Paul among the Postliberals*, 250.

48. Cf. Geoffrey Holsclaw, "Subjects Between Death and Resurrection: Badiou, Žižek, and St. Paul," in *Paul, Philosophy, and the Theopolitical Vision: Critical Engagements with Agamben, Badiou, Žižek, and Others*, ed. Douglas Harink (Eugene, OR: Cascade Books, 2010), 173. Holsclaw largely ignores the role of powers in Paul's conception of the human subject but helpfully engages St. Paul's thought in relation to human subjects and a complex relational field.

49. Cf. Harink, *Paul among the Postliberals*, 249–50; and Giorgio Agamben, *The Time That Remains: A Commentary on the Letter to the Romans*, trans. Patricia Dailey (Stanford, CA: Stanford University Press, 2005), 91.

Christian witness cannot avoid addressing the person in complex entanglement in and with the powers of this world. It is, in fact, the only way to know a person and the only place to address a neighbor.

This talk of "powers" leads us directly to the second danger for apologetics. Christian apologetics always has the potential to be captivated by the powers of the prevailing culture and to participate in or perpetrate what may be called systemic or ideological violence. This is perhaps an even more insidious form of apologetic violence because it is generally invisible. It permeates our everyday practices and beliefs, and lurks just below the surface. This violence, Kierkegaard warns, happens to individual persons in modern societies where genius is supreme and scientific reason is the highest standard.[50] He calls it "the spirit of leveling."[51] As we saw earlier, modern society is populated by free, autonomous, rational individuals. And the place where the members of modern society "meet" to exercise their rational autonomy is the so-called public square, which is imagined to be free not only of political and religious powers but also of the violence associated with them. Yet what happens, Kierkegaard notes, is that this public square depends upon a "leveling" in which all differences are suppressed, ignored, and repressed, as individual persons are nihilistically absorbed into "the public."[52] This "public" has its own spectral ethos. It creates a web of beliefs, perceptions, and values—in short, an ideology—which functions to superficially support the claims (or truths) of public opinion in order to protect the status quo.[53] Kierkegaard therefore aptly characterizes "the public" as "a monstrous abstraction, an all-encompassing something that is nothing" which destroys a person's individuality and threatens even the very ability to act as oneself.[54] And he notes the close connection between the power-elites in modern society who control public

50. We see this critique throughout Kierkegaard's writing, but I thinking especially of *Two Ages: The Age of Revolution and the Present Age. A Literary Review*, ed. and trans. Howard V. Hong and Edna H. Hong (Princeton: Princeton University Press, 1978); and *The Book on Adler*, ed. and trans. Howard V. Hong and Edna H. Hong (Princeton: Princeton University Press, 2009).

51. Kierkegaard, *Two Ages*, 90.

52. Ibid., 90–96.

53. Ibid., 100.

54. Ibid., 91.

opinion (often through the media) and those beliefs that society accepts as true.[55]

Much later than Kierkegaard, Michel Foucault also makes the link between power and truth in what he refers to as a "'general politics' of truth."[56] Foucault argues "truth is a thing of this world"[57] and all our (so-called) truths are therefore constructed by social and political forces. As we saw earlier, our claims to truth have an ideological dimension, because if a statement is to count as a "truth," we need first to have a procedure for making that determination and a final court of appeal to decide on it. Ultimately, every exercise of human reason is embedded in the social practices of a society. Once we establish or make "truths" this way, it quickly becomes "a regime of truth," and as Walsh and Keesmaat explain, these "will determine what kind of discourse might function as true, how one will establish and sanction truth within such a discourse, which techniques will be authorized as legitimate paths to truth, and how the truth-tellers within the regime will be regarded."[58] What seems to matter most to Foucault and Kierkegaard is that the provisional truths we hold always occur within a matrix of social and political power, of which they are both a function. Insofar as the regime needs truth to legitimate it, the regime has a vested interest in keeping truth under its control so as to maintain power. If we look at our claims to truth this way, defending truths made within these regimes can become virtually indistinguishable from ideology and will often take the form of propping up or attempting to legitimize oppressive practices, beliefs, and attitudes by making them "reasonable."[59]

It is little wonder, then, that Kierkegaard suggests Christianity is worse off in the hands of the modern apologists than the man from

55. Ibid., 90–91.

56. Michel Foucault, *Power/Knowledge: Selected Interviews and Other Writings, 1972–1977*, ed. Colin Gordon (New York: Pantheon, 1980), 131.

57. Ibid., 131.

58. See Brian J. Walsh and Sylvia C. Keesmaat, *Colossians Remixed: Subverting the Empire* (Downers Grove, IL: InterVarsity, 2004), 102–05.

59. We do not have to see Foucault's account as negating truth of the sort I have described. He has merely described the conditions in which we arrive at our contingent truth claims and the context in which we attest to truths and are built up by them. What his account does place in jeopardy is the notion of an absolute objective truth. He has also highlighted some of the ways in which our truth claims may be *un*edifying.

Jericho who fell among thieves.[60] By making Christianity "reasonable" they destroy the possibility of Christianity having any credible way to challenge the ideological violence of modern society or build up those who are disaffected by its leveling processes. The amnesia of the modern apologetic project described earlier functions often to blind Christians even to the possibility of this form of violence. Our way of thinking about and practicing Christianity is taken to be the most natural and obvious way of being Christian, and the idea that this might be destructive or unhelpful to others—particularly those in other cultures—may rarely even occur to us. We then overlook real people and proclaim to them the truths of the gospel packaged in "universal" concepts and categories (as well as practices) to which they cannot relate in any personal way and which have often played some role in their mistreatment or exploitation.

This second type of apologetic violence, then, occurs when our Christian witness unwittingly participates in the kind of systemic or ideological violence that takes place in modern rational societies. The values, beliefs, concepts, and even the categories we use to understand and interpret the world are all part of a system (or ideology) that generates destructive attitudes and patterns of behavior such as racism and sexual discrimination, but is always already operative before we are consciously aware of it. This is what enables "good" and "honest" Belgians to allow the naturalization of their fellow human beings (like Kenzo's father) and enables Canadians, who see themselves as morally and spiritually upright in every other way, to tolerate the programmatic elimination of a people's culture and language. This violence is almost completely objective in the sense that it is not attributable to any one person or group and their evil intentions.[61] It is largely anonymous. No one (in particular) is doing it, but it is the underlying violence required to maintain the status quo in which we all participate indirectly.

There is a surprising and subtle way that this modern "spirit of leveling" inserts itself into the apologetic theology of modern Christianity.

60. Kierkegaard, *Book on Adler*, 40. For the story of the man who fell among thieves, see the New Testament account of Jesus's parable of the Good Samaritan in Luke 10:30–37, which is told in response to a lawyer's question about how to identify his neighbor. Cf. Westphal, *Kierkegaard's Critique of Reason and Society*, 22.
61. Slavoj Žižek, *Violence: Six Sideways Reflections* (New York: Picador, 2008), 13.

Often it occurs not on the front lines, so to speak, when we are engaging "the unbeliever" directly with the gospel, but in our attempts to create solidarity among people groups by treating them all under the universal banner of "humanity." Allow me to revert for a moment to my earlier Star Trek illustration. Modern society, I claim, tries to imagine not only itself but the entire human world as a single community—much like the United Federation of Planets with its Prime Directive. There are no boundaries on the rational public square, and there is room in the Federation for every rational species, culture, and language group in all the communities in every country on every planet—that is, so long as they conform to group consensus and charter constitution.[62]

The same is true for much of modern Christian theology.[63] The different ways people engage in worship are (re)conceived as different instances of "religion" that are particular expressions of the common search for the divine. So we continue to believe that any truly rational theology or account of the divine must proceed from premises everyone agrees upon to a conclusion that is rationally demonstrated to the satisfaction of all. And the way to solve theological difference, which has (it is believed) been the cause of the majority of wars and violence, is to bring all the world's beliefs and religions to a common table and affirm them together in their difference—to create a religious version of Star Trek's United Federation of Planets.

The operating assumption in this approach to religious pluralism, as William Placher notes, is that "the great religious traditions" are

62. This is what makes first the Klingons and later the Romulons the enemies of the Federation. They do not comply with the universal charter and therefore—as the "other"—are fair game. It is significant to note that Klingons later become Federation allies once they accept the charter. An irony therefore emerges when one compares the way the Federation relates to "others" and the infamous Borg (technically the "Cyborg"), the pseudo-race of cybernetic organisms whose mission is to "assimilate" all other life-forms into their half-biological, half-machine existence as a means of "achieving perfection." As it turns out, this appears to be a mirror image of what the Federation does at the sociological level. The very thing feared most by the Starship Enterprise's captain, Jean-Luc Picard—who himself was temporarily "assimilated" by the Borg—is an obscene image of himself.

63. One of the best places I can think of to begin a Christian theology of other religions is William C. Placher, *Unapologetic Theology: A Christian Voice in a Pluralistic Conversation* (Louisville: Westminster John Knox, 1989). My account here is very similar to Placher's.

really just "different ways of conceiving and experiencing the one ultimate divine reality."[64] This way it is possible to understand every religious belief and practice as the local embodiment of a common interstellar quest, moving toward a single goal—so that religious expressions are various manifestations of a single phenomenon called "religion."[65] Here the modern spirit of leveling tries to imagine all the worshipping communities of the various human societies as another kind of "public" in which rational consensus replaces personal piety as the vehicle of truth. But this precludes both the possibility of prophetic witness and, as Placher argues, any serious dialogue between persons from different religious traditions:

> *Serious* dialogue [between persons of different religious faiths] indeed requires openness to change, but it also demands a sense of how significant changing one's faith would be. . . . Arguments for openness can encourage an ideal of occupying many different positions which then becomes a surrogate for the old dream of occupying no particular position at all. If we are honest, we will admit that we stand somewhere. If we are serious, we will feel serious commitments to the place we stand.[66]

To do otherwise is disingenuous and patronizing. It is a false universal and ultimately a kind of violence. We are like the Western Buddhist who "tries out" Buddhism to see if it works (relieves stress, provides some needed self-discipline, or provides a general sense of well-being). Or we are like the academic religionist who critiques the Christian missionary movement in the Canadian Arctic on the grounds that it involved a cultural transformation as the indigenous Inuit people stopped worshipping their traditional gods. The problem, of course, is that in cases like these genuine believers do not understand themselves from the perspective of modern pluralism. It is not only that the modern characterization of religious practice is the imposition of an outsider's perspective, but more significantly it fails to take seriously the notion that religious beliefs are concerned

---

64. Ibid., 16. He is quoting John Hick, *The Problems of Religious Pluralism* (New York: St. Martin's Press, 1985), 102, as representative of this sort of theological perspective.
65. Cf. Placher, *Unapologetic Theology*, 17.
66. Ibid., 149.

with the question of being in the truth. Believers *believe*.[67] They do not see themselves (just) as increasing their personal enjoyment or (merely) engaging in cultural traditions. They engage in the beliefs and practices of their "religion" because they believe them to be the path to truth. A Buddhist in Tibet is not trying relieve stress, and an Inuit does not visit an *angakkuq* (spiritual guide or healer) to strengthen their connection to tribal identity by maintaining cultural practices (though this is, in fact, an important part of what is going on). These believers are engaging in spiritual practices for their edification. In short, they wish to be in the truth.[68]

The important thing to realize is that this religious leveling of modernity is yet another version of ideological violence. So, right at the point where much of modern Christianity believes itself to be most magnanimous, it is actually perpetrating a form of ideological violence. Its witness therefore fails to be gospel—the *good news*.

The lesson of apologetic violence is that there is more than one way to deny Christ in modernity.[69] There is the straightforward way of the atheist who openly confesses to disbelief in God, takes offense at the gospel, and leaves aside Christian belief as superstitious and irrational; or it may be done indirectly, perhaps even with sincerity, by a Christian who uses the objective truths of Christianity to do things that are themselves unloving and unedifying. But there is also the seemingly more sophisticated (and often heterodox) way of the modern thinker who openly professes Christian belief precisely because it is the highest expression of human reason—which also

67. This is true even in modernity and postmodernity, where faith is very fragile. I define faith, you will recall, as a return to the naïveté or directness of belief.

68. This is the point of all great spiritual theologies. Thomas Merton, for instance, tells us that the point of true spirituality—Christian and otherwise—is an "ascent to truth," and that "The Truth" [*sic*] to which Christian contemplation unites us "is not an abstraction but a Reality and Life." For Merton, this involves a detachment from "the world" and "the things of this life" which spin "a whole net of falsities" around a person's spirit. See Thomas Merton, *The Ascent to Truth* (New York: Harcourt Brace Jovanovich, 1951), 23. Interestingly, on the the cover of the Continuum edition of Merton's *Ascent to Truth*, The Dalai Lama writes on the cover that this book was the first time he had ever encountered "such a feeling of spirituality by anyone who professed Christianity."

69. Westphal describes Kierkegaard's critique of apologetics in these same terms. *Kierkegaard's Critique of Reason and Society*, 23–24.

turns out to be the authoritative voice of the established order and is therefore a distortion of the gospel. In this situation, Merold Westphal observes, the crucial question to ask regards the *kind* of social order our apologetics authorizes. And the answer to this question reveals whether or not our appeal to human reason is a byword "to obscure our creation of God in our own image," which we then use to "serve as the cosmic validator of our institutions and life-styles."[70] When this happens, our witness ceases to be edifying and therefore ceases to be truth. And Kierkegaard, at least, will call for a moratorium on apologetics.[71]

Conclusion

The ethics of witness has now landed us squarely in the territory of a politics of witness. Looking back to the two stories at the beginning of this chapter, one can see that a defense of the objectivity of Christian truths in *those* situations may make it very difficult for those receiving the witness not to hear in them an implicit justification for the wrong that has been done to them by the established powers. The kind of politics operative here might be called *deep* politics, however, for I am not talking about leveraging power within some structure of governance. I am speaking at a more profound level of the relations that exist between persons that constitute them as a people—the level at which values and purposes give rise to explicit political structures that govern the relations between persons and how they conduct their common life together. Deep politics concerns public power and power-relations between private persons.

So when I say the prophetic witness is political, I mean the concern about ideological or systemic apologetic violence connects Christian witness to the issues of deep politics. Against modern apologetics, a postmodern prophetic witness acknowledges that *there is no space outside political power* in which we can persuade people. The deep politics of modernity allows modern apologetics to imagine itself as operating *apolitically*, as dealing only with the rational justifications

70. Ibid., 24.
71. Cf. ibid., 27.

for objective truths, and therefore as concerned only with the private, religious beliefs of individuals. It is "a politics of the privileged" that thrives in the context of Western academic elitism (and those from other places and religions trained by Western elites).[72] This is possible because modern society imagines the self as existing over against its relations to others and one's personal convictions as having nothing (or little) to do with public policy. And so the dream of modern apologetics is that its arguments and propositions—as objective truths—are timeless, universal, and neutral and may function in any social context without a basic challenge to the governing structures (except in those cases where the existing polity expressly forbids Christian beliefs and practices) and without violence to the individual person. Against this, the prophetic witness I advocate understands persuasion, reason, and witness to be political acts in the sense they are public (or interpersonal) acts that always and fundamentally concern persons—their identities, their relations, and the powers at work on, in, and through them. The witness brings personal commitments into public space, and places every society in question, along with the powers that generate its status quo and have vested interests in keeping the private and public spheres separate.

It is ironic, then, that the deep politics of prophetic witness is also what makes the prophetic stance appear politically ambivalent according to the surface politics of particular governmental or institutional

72. Harink, *Paul among the Postliberals*, 245. Harink cites Kenneth Surin, who states:

> Only someone who is not aware of the always particular "location" from which he or she theorizes can celebrate the new "global city" and propound a world or global theology in this apparently unreflective way: impoverished peasants from Kedah in Malaysia find it well-nigh impossible to accept that they and a wealthy landowner *from their own village* are situated in the same moral or social location, and yet we are urged by [modern theologians of religious pluralism] to believe that such Malay peasants, their landlord and even the Duke of Westminster or the Hunt brothers inhabit the same global city or share a common human history. . . . The discourses of religious pluralism . . . effectively incorporates, and thereby dissolves, the localized and oppositional "spaces" of people like peasants in Malaysia. Local attachments, with their always specific histories and politics, are displaced and dispersed by a global and "globalizing" topography as the local is subsumed under the regime of universal ("A 'Politics of Speech': Religious Pluralism in the Age of the McDonald's Hamburger," in *Christian Uniqueness Reconsidered: The Myth of a Pluralistic Theology Reconsidered*, ed. Gavin D'Costa [Maryknoll, NY: Orbis, 1990], 203–4).

systems—while the opposite is so often true in modern apologetics. Often, modern Christians are politically engaged in the surface politics of modern society, fighting the so-called culture wars with very clearly marked political boundary lines, but all the while they are unreflective about the deep politics at work.[73] The prophetic stance of Christian witness I am after cannot be identified with political partisanship to any ruling parties, plans, or ideals. The deep political requirement of Christian witness is love, and its primary goal, is person-preserving and not to produce any particular kind of society or particular program of action. The prophetic stance of the Christian witness, then, is an attitude, a way of facing society and engaging programs of action.[74] To be wedded to any particular society or program of action indissolubly subverts the prophetic thrust of witness as that which stands against the powers that stand against the truth.

As we saw from our earlier discussions of the truth of witness, the ability to witness requires a community of like-minded people whose way of life together displays the truth being witnessed to and makes sense of the witnesses' speech. It takes a community to tell the truth. This is what may be called a socially embodied witness that

73. A key dimension of the deep politics of modernity can be understood in terms of its primary allegiance to the modern notion of universal human rights as spelled out in the United Nations' Universal Declaration of Human Rights (available online at http://www.un.org/en/documents/udhr/), which carries much of the theoretical freight brokering the theoretical gap between the "private" individual and the so-called public square in terms that are universal, neutral, and objective. As Žižek has already pointed out, Christians who want to trade punches in this arena do not seem to realize that they are caught in a catch-22 such that there is no way for them to win. It is structurally impossible, he argues, in the deep politics of human rights to draw a clear line of separation between the "misuse" of a right and the "proper" use—"that is, the use that does *not* violate the Commandments." Slavoj Žižek, *The Fragile Absolute—Or, Why Is the Christian Legacy Worth Fighting For?* (New York: Verso, 2000), 111. In this context, the discourse of human rights is juxtaposed against God's commandments precisely as the right to *break* them: commandments are inherently transgressive of private rights because they do not recognize the basic distinction between public and private. Žižek's point is not that the discourse of human rights directly encourages the breaking of God's law but that it fights to maintain a shady "grey zone" that remains out of reach of religious and political power, so that "if power probes into it, catching me with my pants down and trying to prevent my violations, I can cry: 'Assault on my basic human Rights!'" (110–11).

74. Cf. Glenn Tinder, *The Political Meaning of Christianity: An Interpretation* (Baton Rouge, LA: Louisiana State University Press, 1989), 8.

gives content to the claims of witness and creates the possibility for their making any sense at all.[75] The communal shape of this witness is structurally identical to the prophetic shape of the person who witnesses. That is, the church—as the community of witnesses—depends no less on the Word of God than on the call of the individual witness. They are "called out" (the literal meaning of the Greek word, *ekklēsia*, used for "church" in the New Testament) as a new people, called out and constituted as such by the Holy Spirit in a way that cuts across the "natural" boundaries of ethnicity, language, race, culture, and every other way that humans differentiate and divide themselves from each other. To be called into the church, to confess Jesus as Lord, is to be called to the fellowship of a new vocation that completely reorients, reorders, and reprioritizes every other calling or facet of a person's life.[76] The significance of this point is that to be a prophetic witness is also political in the more profound sense of bringing one into conflict with all other commitments to the powers and institutions of one's society. To confess the Christian gospel and to be edified by it is at the same time to be called into a distinct way of being—a manner of being-with-others—that constitutes the church as God's people. Subsequently, there is an apocalyptic element to the truth that edifies the Christian, which interrupts and disrupts the truth-regimes of worldly societies and gives rise to a stance that is engaged and concerned in the affairs of this world, but is also hesitant and critical at the same time.[77]

75. This is an internal coherence, not a universal one. I am therefore stopping short of Alasdair MacIntyre's concept of a "socially embodied *argument*" by which the rational merits of a living tradition may be judged. MacIntyre's idea is that a particular vision of the Good Life—the human *telos*—is inherent in the practices of a given tradition and is thereby made publically observable and can therefore be rationally evaluated in universal terms. See Alasdair MacIntyre, *After Virtue: A Study in Moral Theory*, 2nd ed. (Notre Dame, IN: University of Notre Dame Press, 1984), 222.

76. Cf. Agamben's discussion of the messianic "*hōs mē*" in Paul's letter to the Romans. *The Time That Remains*, 23–26, and his section regarding "The Cut of Appelles" (49–57).

77. Cf. Tinder, *The Political Meaning of Christianity*, 8. Cf. also Douglas Harink, "Introduction: From Apocalypse to Philosophy—and Back," in *Paul, Philosophy, and the Theopolitical Vision: Critical Engagements with Agamben, Badiou, Žižek, and Others*, ed. Douglas Harink (Eugene, OR: Cascade Books, 2010), 2.

So Richard Rorty and other postmodernists concerned about violence and oppression are not entirely wrong to be troubled by the notion of truth, because truth, even as edification, always involves a violent upheaval of some sort. At its deepest level, truth is prophetic, and this means it often is *traumatic*. Truth profoundly interrupts and disturbs our patterns of self-reliance and our staid interpretations of the world (i.e., our traditions). Because they depend upon a rupture with our preconceived notions of self-adequacy and human sufficiency, the truths of prophetic witness potentially place us at odds with, first, ourselves and, second, our community.[78] Truth undoes or compromises the easy confidence we have in ourselves and our received beliefs, so that faithfulness to ourselves and our traditions often takes the form of questioning our ability to account for our world. I am placed in question by the Truth, and I in turn place the practices and beliefs of my community in question.

A Christian witness has a dialectical relation with tradition as one who has *received* these truths but must come to own them and believe them personally. A Christian witness is one who been "apocalypsed"[79] by the truth, if I can use that language, one who has been undone—and redone—by encountering the One who is Truth; and this has reordered the witness's beliefs, perceptions, and practices and has made everything else relative to this event. (This echoes St. Paul's way of talking about his encounter with Jesus Messiah.) And for this reason the Christian hermeneutical tradition is never and can never

78. Here I am stopping just short of speaking of the trauma of truth in terms of the "event" that reorients our entire symbolic representation of the world, as Žižek, *The Fragile Absolute*, 92–107, describes it—and similarly Alain Badiou, *Saint Paul: The Foundation of Universalism*, trans. Ray Brassier (Stanford, CA: Stanford University Press, 2003), passim. What Žižek and Badiou call the truth event, I identify as the in-breaking of Truth (God) into human cultures, languages, and practices. I certainly do not wish to deny the function of truth that Žižek and Badiou describe, but I am taking a wider application of the concept of truth.

79. I first heard this term used as a verb by Douglas Harink on February 7, 2010, in a lecture titled "Paul's Political Gospel," delivered at The Anglican Parish of Christ Church, Diocese of Edmonton, Alberta. Ryan Hansen also uses the term in Ryan L. Hansen, "Messianic or Apocalyptic? Engaging Agamben on Paul and Politics," in *Paul, Philosophy, and the Theopolitical Vision*, 198–226. See Douglas Harink, "Time and Politics in Four Commentaries on Romans," in *Paul, Philosophy, and the Theopolitical Vision*, 296–304, and Harink, *Paul among the Postliberals*, 67–103, for Harink's discussion of apocalypse in Paul's thought.

function as just another expression of modern reason. It does not rely on geniuses who have the power to grasp and own the truth for themselves. This is precisely what Kierkegaard is trying to draw out when he distinguishes between genius as the modern source of warrant and the Christian apostle, who operates from revelation. One who has been edified by the truth has also been dislocated by it and has been (or is going) through the violent process of being remade by something that is beyond the self.[80]

So when I say that as a Christian I stand in a dialectical relationship with my tradition, I mean that I am *shaped by* it and also that I am a *shaper of* the tradition. My role as a shaper of tradition, however, is not a function of my genius but rather is due to the fact that I personally have been gripped by the truth that is at the same time the source and goal of the tradition.

For this reason, the prophetic speech of a Christian witness is conspicuously impolitic.[81] Because the prophetic witness has been edified by the truth and has, in this sense, heard from God (albeit the God known through the Hebrew-Christian Scriptures and the language and practices of that tradition), the witness to truth has a place from which to stand both within Christian tradition, as a representative of it, and outside it, calling it back to faithfulness. What is also true of prophets, then, is that while they challenge and even speak against their traditions, they are also more deeply committed to them than those who are comfortable in the status quo.[82] It is precisely *because* they are so committed to their tradition and believe in its deepest impulses that prophets sometimes attack it. The prophetic call is always to a deeper fidelity to the founding event of the tradition, but not in such a way that controls it or even tries to make it into a univocal, monochromatic tradition.[83]

80. But in this a person does not, as the Kierkegaardian pseudonym Judge William points out, "become someone other than he was before, but he becomes *himself*" (my emphasis). Søren Kierkegaard, *Either/Or*, part 2, ed. and trans. Howard V. Hong and Edna H. Hong (Princeton: Princeton University Press, 1987), 177.
81. Westphal, *Kierkegaard's Critique of Reason and Society*, 14.
82. Cf. ibid., 15.
83. There is a sense in which I am in basic agreement with Žižek, *Fragile Absolute*, 92–93 (and elsewhere), who, similar to Badiou et al., speaks about the messianic event of the resurrection of Jesus as the founding gesture of a Truth that opens up a new possibility for imagining the Real. For Žižek an "event" is an indeterminate (and

Here we have come full circle, as it were, for it is now possible to see how, in the wake of the so-called Enlightenment project and its concept of reason, my proposal for a postmodern witness is different from Alasdair MacIntyre's options rehearsed in the introduction. As I suggested in my introduction, unless we are to continue with the Enlightenment project, MacIntyre believes we must choose either Aristotle or Nietzsche—either a tradition-based concept of rationality or a subversion of reason (like Foucault's) based on the "will to power."[84] I opt for neither "either" nor "or." The reasons of faith do not (necessarily) make an integrated whole that is open to "public" inspection, and my postmodern witness is willing to submit to a "heaven-sent insanity" over a human-made sanity.[85] But my concept of Christian witness does not give up on the task of reason-giving nor truth nor even truth-telling just because it knows that every truth to which the witness testifies is contingent and made from within a matrix of social power. I have tried hard not to pit the failure to believe Christian truth against reason (rationality), as if the primary breakdown is *rational*.

---

indeterminable) rupture in an existing Structural Order that both inaugurates a system of truths and operates as its "obscene supplement." What is important to this concept of the "event" is its utter singularity and uniqueness so that it transforms "individuals into subjects universally, irrespectively of their race, sex, social class [etc.]." Slavoj Žižek, *The Ticklish Subject: The Absent Centre of Political Ontology* (New York: Verso, 1999), 142. Perhaps one way of looking at this is to say that "events" found traditions or ways of systematizing and understanding life, the world, and everything in it on the basis of something like a revelatory and life-changing experience—an apocalyptic moment of truth.

84. See MacIntyre, *After Virtue*, especially the chapter "Nietzsche or Aristotle?" 109–20. He develops this thesis throughout his subsequent work and eventually replaces Aristotle with Aquinas. See Alasdair MacIntyre, *Whose Justice? Which Rationality?* (Notre Dame, IN: University of Notre Dame Press, 1988); and Alasdair MacIntyre, *Three Rival Versions of Moral Inquiry* (Notre Dame, IN: University of Notre Dame Press, 1990). In *Three Rival Versions*, MacIntyre identifies our options for rational discourse as (roughly): (1) *encyclopaedia*, the modern form of reason which tries to subsume everything in a universal discourse; (2) *genealogy*, the Nietzschean response that subverts any notion of a universal rational discourse by viewing all rational discourse as (subjective) exercises of power; and (3) *tradition*, the Aristotelian-Thomistic form of rational discourse embodied in a tradition that survives over time by overcoming the rational limitations of its rivals and predecessors.

85. Westphal, *Kierkegaard's Critique of Reason and Society*, 86, uses this Socratic phrase from the *Phaedrus* to link Kierkegaard's critique of modern reason to the Socratic critique.

I am angling, in other words, for another option: an alternative to MacIntyre's forms of rational inquiry that might be called *apocalyptic* (in the sense it is disruptive of and subversive to any notions of the self-sufficiency and adequacy of human reason) and stresses the priority of the transcendent, reorienting nature of truth (versus an immanent, universalizing function of reason). Reason's function, then, is not to ground our truths but to explain them. Reason depends on a (logically) prior Truth to situate it. This view of reason positions it somewhere between MacIntyre's options, as tradition is important to rational discourse but is outstripped by a personal relation to truth that is never (fully) under reason's control. Just as St. Augustine argues that Aristotle's virtues are, for the Christian, mere "glittering vices" (insofar as they are a form of self-reliance and self-sufficiency), so I argue for MacIntyre's Aristotelian view of reason.[86] The temptation for the Christian is to allow the fact that reason comes to us through others and is confirmed by them to somehow act as a substitute for hearing from God, to reduce faith to the staid reasons of an interpretive community. Instead, I want to linger in that liminal space William Lane Craig identifies (and then immediately feels the need to escape from) as the impulse to cling to Christ even if reason turns against you. Ultimately, what I find decisive for the Christian witness is not what is *reasonable*, what the crowd tells one to believe or to say, but the voice of God—"a wisdom whose secret is foolishness" and a "hope whose form is madness."[87] When this is forgotten, suppressed, or denied and God's existence (along with the rest of faith's affirmations) is made out to rest confidently on the processes of human reason, we should look for the specter of Judas lurking somewhere nearby.

86. This connects, Kierkegaard would say, to the New Testament's insistence that the opposite of sin is not virtue but *faith*. Our being good is not a matter (ultimately) of our rational control, while at the same time making it clear that *with* faith spiritual discipline profits much. See Søren Kierkegaard, *The Sickness Unto Death: A Christian Psychological Exposition for Upbuilding and Awakening*, ed. and trans. Howard V. Hong and Edna H. Hong (Princeton: Princeton University Press, 1980), 82, 46.
87. Westphal draws attention to these phrases from Kierkegaard, which Kierkegaard uses to describe the faith that makes Abraham "the greatest of all" men. Søren Kierkegaard, *Fear and Trembling*, ed. and trans. Howard V. Hong and Edna H. Hong (Princeton: Princeton University Press, 1983), 16–17.

So where does all this leave us? I trust it leaves us with the hope and the means to confess the truth of Jesus as Lord faithfully in these postmodern times. My aim in this book is to place us in a position to acknowledge the topsy-turvy fragmentation of our (post)modern world that has gone down the rabbit hole with Alice, without trying to deny or suppress the unsettling nature of our contemporary situation. I think it can be shown that it is a fundamental mistake for us, at this juncture, to carry forward the modern paradigm and mount a damage control operation that attempts to make sense of and control the chaos by reconstructing Christian belief in terms amenable to the modern epistemological project. We are not going to be able to reason ourselves back to paradise. But at the same time, I trust this book leaves us with enough of a prophetic witness to the truth of Jesus Christ that we are edified and built up without trying to pretend that modernity never happened and then setting about the business of reconstructing the order of the premodern world. My confidence is that the broken fragments of the premodern mirror may yet be used to reflect the beauty of Jesus in ten thousand places and many, many thousands-upon-millions of more faces.

Epilogue

In the conclusion of *Concluding Unscientific Postscript to Philosophical Fragments*, Kierkegaard tells this story:

> It is said to have chanced in England that a man was attacked on the highway by a robber who had made himself unrecognizable by wearing a big wig. He falls upon the traveler, seizes him by the throat and shouts, "Your purse!" He gets the purse and keeps it, but the wig he throws away. A poor man comes along the same road, puts it on and arrives at the next town where the traveler had already denounced the crime, he is arrested, is recognized by the traveler, who takes his oath that he is the man. By chance, the robber is present in the courtroom, sees the misunderstanding, turns to the judge and says, "It seems to me that the traveler has regard rather to the wig than to the man," and he asks permission to make a trial. He puts on the wig, seizes the traveler by the throat, crying, "Your purse!"—and the traveler recognizes the robber and offers to swear to it—the only trouble is that already he has taken an oath.
>
> So it is, in one way or another, with every man who has a "what" and is not attentive to the "how": he swears, he takes his oath, he runs errands, he ventures life and blood, he is executed—all on account of the wig.[1]

---

1. Søren Kierkegaard, *Concluding Unscientific Postscript to Philosophical Fragments*, 2 vols., ed. and trans. Howard V. Hong and Edna H. Hong (Princeton: Princeton University Press, 1992), 1.616.

And so also, I am tempted to say, it is with all those who possess a seemingly coherent set of rational, well-justified, well-argued Christian beliefs, but do not allow themselves *or anyone else* to be edified by them. Such beliefs may be reassuring, they may be intellectually satisfying, and they may even "preach good," but in the end the person who holds them will have missed the one thing that was necessary. All on account of the "wig."

Index

175

ethics of, 139–48
to gospel, 83–84, 120
irony in, 92–96
as political, 18
professionalization of, 82
and prophets, 115–16
and truth, 101–2, 106–7, 124
Wittgenstein, Ludwig, 74n62, 117–18

worldview, 3, 41, 80
of Christianity, 25, 34–35, 45–46, 106
of Enlightenment, 8, 28, 48
of premodernity, 6

Yoder, John Howard, 105

Žižek, Slavoj, 47, 125, 126n38, 165n73,
168–69n83